Avro Mil
1910-63

Books

AVIATION INDUSTRY SERIES, VOLUME 3

Front cover image: The last Vulcan to serve the RAF was XH558, which kept the giant bomber flying with the Vulcan Display Flight until 1993 when the 'bean counters' decided it was time to call it a day! (Via *Aeroplane*)

Title page image: The pristine Battle of Britain Memorial Flight's Lancaster PA474. (Martyn Chorlton)

Contents page image: There is no doubting that the Avro Manchester was let down by its undeveloped Vulture engines, but from a handling point of view, the bomber drew nothing but praise from its pilots. A 207 Squadron pilot demonstrates this trait after tail chasing a 44 Squadron Hampden over Waddington in November 1941. (*Aeroplane*)

Published by Key Books
An imprint of Key Publishing Ltd
PO Box 100
Stamford
Lincs PE19 1XQ

www.keypublishing.com

Original edition published as *Aeroplane's Avro Company Profile 1910–1963 (Military)* © 2013, edited by Martyn Chorlton

This edition © 2022

ISBN 978 1 80282 380 6

Typeset by SJmagic DESIGN SERVICES, India.

Contents

Introduction

Founded in 1910 by Alliott Verdon Roe, A. V. Roe and Company Limited built its first military aircraft two years later. By 1914, the company was literally flying when it designed the first of many iconic aircraft in the shape of the Avro 504, which sold in colossal numbers and was the key factor in keeping the company in the aviation industry after the end of World War One, while many others fell by the wayside. Production of the 504 continued into the 1920s and, despite this lean period, orders were secured for the Aldershot and Bison, but by the end of the 1920s, it was the Tutor that saw the production lines fill to capacity again.

Avro was by now established at Newton Heath, Hamble and Woodford, but with Alliott's departure in 1928, the future of the company looked to be in the north. With war looming again, new military designs gained momentum, although another huge success, in the shape of the Anson, was germinated from a requirement for Imperial Airways. In 1936, Avro became part of the new Hawker Siddeley group and within two years was operating a new factory at Chadderton where, together with Newton Heath, all focus was on building the Anson, Blenheim and later the Manchester. Following production of just 200 Manchesters, attention turned to one of the greatest bombers of World War Two: the Lancaster, of which over 7,300 were built. This caused further expansion at Woodford, part use of Ringway and a 'shadow' factory at Yeadon under Avro control throughout the war years.

Although an obvious contraction of orders took place during the post-war years, Avro was, thanks to its earlier successes, a big player in the British aviation industry and would continue to produce an iconic range of military aircraft. On the back of the Lancaster, the Lincoln and Shackleton were ordered in large numbers for the RAF and the most famous jet-powered delta bomber of all, the Vulcan, kept the company at the forefront. However, the long-term plan of reducing the number of aircraft manufacturers first envisaged in the 1930s began to take hold in the 1960s, when British Aircraft Corporation (BAC) and Hawker Siddeley encompassed all of the country's surviving companies.

The last hurrah was the delightful 748, which just scrapes into this publication as the final example of an aircraft solely designed by Avro. Many of these aircraft are in museums across the world, testimony to what they achieved, the men who flew them and the great aircraft manufacturer that designed and built them.

Avro Lancaster Mk I R5689 of 50 Squadron is loaded with bombs for the benefit of the press at RAF Swinderby in August 1942. (*Aeroplane*)

The Avro Military Story

Sealing the deal for a pound!

A determined Edwin Alliott Verdon Roe was adamant that there was a future in flying machines from a very early stage, although this forward-thinking was not shared by many at the turn of 20th century. Roe had already entered into business with J.A.P engine designer, J. A. Prestwick on 15 September 1908, but the J.A.P. Avroplane Company was amicably dissolved by November 1909, following a disagreement over the design of a Triplane.

Undeterred, Roe was lucky to be surrounded by a supportive family, including his father, Dr Edwin Hodson Roe, and his brother, Humphrey Verdon Roe, who owned H. W. Everard and Company, both of whom lent him money. The latter agreement with his brother was taken one stage further when, on 27 April 1909, Alliott and Humphrey entered into a partnership in a deal that was sealed with a payment of £1! With this crucial foundation block laid, A. V. Roe and Company was officially formed on 1 January 1910.

Gaining a foothold

Alliott's first workshops were established at the Everard factory at Brownsfield Mills, Ancoats, Manchester, so that Humphrey could keep a close eye on proceedings. Alliott wanted to be closer to London and flight testing of his early aircraft was carried out at Brooklands, where he rented an erecting shed for £100 per year. By 1910, the Avro Flying School was established at Brooklands, only to move to Shoreham the following year, but this opened up the opportunity to fly seaplanes from the River Adur.

The year 1911 saw Alliott still struggling with finances, despite his partnership with Humphrey, and the hunt continued to find a third substantial investor. There was no problem finding private supporters, but when it came to the major players, many of whom were approached, including Sir W. G. Armstrong Whitworth and Company, Crossley Motors and the Sheffield Simpex Motor Car Company, all of them responded with a similar mantra, stating

Sir Alliott Verdon Roe outside Buckingham Palace after receiving his knighthood in 1929. (Via Martyn Chorlton)

A wide variety of subcontractors were drawn into the fledgling aviation industry thanks to the huge orders that Avro received for its 504. This example was built by Frederick Sage and Company Limited located in Walton, Peterborough. (Via Martyn Chorlton)

that aviation was too risky a venture! This left Humphrey as the sole investor and before A. V. Roe and Company became a success, he had pumped in £10,000.

By 1912, the company was beginning to find its feet, bolstered financially by an investment of £30,000 from brewing magnate James Grimble Groves, and as a result, A. V. Roe became a limited company on 11 January 1913. A move to new workshops at Clifton Street, Miles Platting, Manchester, followed in April 1913 and A. V. Roe and Company Limited (or Avro for short) was on its way.

The first of many military machines

Avro's first military venture began in 1911, with a demanding specification from the War Office for a new biplane. The Avro Type 500 and 502 (aka the Type E) was the company's first aircraft built in numbers, albeit only 14 in total; all of them went on to serve with the fledgling Royal Flying Corps (RFC) and Royal Naval Air Service (RNAS). This significant aeroplane was developed into one of the world's most iconic aircraft – the Avro 504, a machine that received massive orders thanks to the outbreak of World War One in August 1914.

In response to the immediate success of the 504, Avro had no choice but to expand, the premises at Clifton Street being far too small for large scale production. Clifton Street was destined to be relegated to just being a Woodwork Department, while much larger buildings were rented from the nearby company Mather and Platt, located at Newton Heath off Briscoe Lane. Further land was bought close to the Newton Heath factory, but this would not be developed until 1919.

The Avro 504 was a phenomenal success, not just for Avro but a host of subcontractors, which kept them gainfully employed right up to the Armistice and beyond. These included: the Australian Aircraft and Engineering, Sydney, New South Wales, Australia; Bleriot and SPAD Aircraft Works, Addlestone; The Brush Electrical Engineering Co Ltd, Loughborough; Canadian Aeroplanes Ltd, Toronto, Canada;

The Eastbourne Aviation Co Ltd, Eastbourne; Fabrica Militar de Aviones, Cordoba, Argentina; Frederick Sage and Co Ltd, Peterborough and London; The Grahame-White Aviation Co Ltd, Hendon Aerodrome, London; Harland and Wolff Ltd, Belfast; The Henderson Scottish Aviation Factory, Aberdeen; Hewlett and Blondeau Ltd, Luton; The Humber Motor Co Ltd, Coventry; Morgan and Co, Leighton Buzzard; Nakajima Hikoki Seisaku Sho, Ohta-Machi, Tokyo, Japan; Parnall & Sons, Bristol; Regent Carriage, Fulham; S. E. Saunders Ltd, East Cowes, Isle of Wight; Savages Ltd, King's Lynn; Societe Anonyme Belge de Constructions Aeronautiques Haren, Brussels, Belgium; The Sunbeam Motor Car Co Ltd, Wolverhampton; TNCA, Balbuena field in Mexico City, Mexico; and the Yokosuka Naval Arsenal, Japan. Many of these companies had never built aircraft before and, with the war's end, would never make them again.

Split company

By 1916, Alliott expressed a wish to establish a new testing facility for seaplanes that would require a waterside location. Several different locations were visited in Lancashire and at least one near Brighton, until an ideal site was found at Hamble on the edge of Southampton Water. Alliott had big plans for the Hamble site, which not only included a brand-new purpose-built works but also a garden city for Avro employees. The project progressed to the point of a few hangars and 24 houses before Alliott was forced

Along with Alliott's father, Dr Edwin Hodson Roe, his brother Humphrey, here in uniform when he was an observer with the Royal Flying Corps (RFC), was instrumental in providing the initial financial backing and support that got Avro off the ground. (Via *Aeroplane*)

to bring a halt to proceedings because of the demand for wartime building materials. Hamble would only aspire to being an experimental shop for the remainder of the war under the charge of General Manager R. J. Parrott, who joined Alliott in 1909 as an assistant and draughtsman.

The potential of having an extra works at Hamble caused a great deal of initial excitement within the company, as potentially large orders for the 529 Pike bomber and 530 fighter beckoned. A proposal to split the company into two, by establishing A. V. Roe (Southampton) Ltd, was put into effect on 31 December 1916. The plan was that the Hamble concern would focus on gaining orders for the Type 530, while the Manchester element would focus on the Pike; once orders were achieved, production of both types was to be split between the companies. Frustratingly for Avro, the combination of the curtailed expansion at Hamble and the failure to secure orders for either aircraft brought the whole plan to a close.

Humphrey moves on

Humphrey Verdon Roe left the company on 13 July 1917, having decided to join the RFC. Humphrey's shareholding was now worth £20,875, which gives an indication as to how well Avro was performing at the time. Without even factoring in the money being made from aircraft production, a device known as the Avro Wire-strainer, designed to tension interplane bracing wires, was making an annual profit of £40,000 alone.

As with all manufacturers of military equipment, the Armistice of November 1918 brought an end to this prosperous period, and 504 production, which had already reached just under 9,000 aircraft, was slashed to just a handful of machines. Diversification was now the key to survival and those employees who were lucky enough to keep their jobs after the war were now building baby carriages and billiard tables rather than aircraft.

The 504 still gave the company a foothold in military aviation and chief designer, Roy Chadwick, who first joined Avro in 1911, continued to churn out military designs. By the mid-1920s, having flight tested their aircraft at Alexandra Park for many years, Avro was forced to find a new site. Land at New Hall Farm was purchased, a single hangar established, and the long history of Woodford Aerodrome began. Small production batches for the Royal Air Force (RAF) and refurbishing 504s for foreign air forces kept the company going during the lean 1920s. Various 'one off' military designs helped, but it was the replacement

Roy Chadwick joined Alliott Verdon Roe's fledgling company in 1911 as a personal assistant and draughtsman, later rising to the position of chief designer until his death in 1947. (Aeroplane)

A view looking west over the original Woodford aerodrome site with Ansons and Blenheims parked close to the collection of flight sheds. The area at the upper left of this photograph, disappearing out of view, is now the Woodford Golf Club next to Old Hall Lane. (Via *Aeroplane*)

for the 504 as a primary trainer for the RAF, in the shape of the Tutor, that once again saw Avro's fortunes begin to turn for the better.

Alliott moves on

The late 1920s brought great change for Alliott Verdon Roe, who, in 1928, decided to sell his interest in the company to Sir John Davenport Siddeley of Sir W. G. Armstrong Whitworth Aircraft Ltd. Having already received the OBE in 1920, Alliott was knighted in the 1929 New Year's Honours List. The same year, together with John Lord, Sir Alliott took a controlling interest in the boat-builders S. E. Saunders, the company being renamed Saunders-Roe Ltd (aka SARO). Sir Alliott Verdon remained at the helm of Saunders-Roe until his death at the age of 80 on 4 January 1958.

Take overs

From August 1920, the majority shareholder of Avro was Crossley Motors, which sold its interests in the company to Armstrong Siddeley Holdings Ltd in 1928. After a reshuffle of assets, the design and development department, located at Hamble, was moved north to Manchester, although the Southampton element of the company remained in Avro hands until it was sold to Air Service Training Ltd in April 1931.

Avro now entered another period of prosperity, as orders for both military and civilian aircraft were on the rise. The year 1935 saw the formation of Hawker Siddeley Aircraft Company Limited, which encompassed J. D. Siddeley, Armstrong Siddeley and the aircraft manufacturers Armstrong Whitworth, Hawker and Gloster and Avro as subsidiaries. By the following year, Avro was being guided by a

Inter-war success came for Avro when it won the contract to produce the 504 replacement: the Tutor primary trainer. Some of the more than 400 built are seen here on the production line at Newton Heath in 1935. (Via *Aeroplane*)

mature experienced group of directors, including Roy Chadwick and Roy Dobson, the latter having joined Avro back in 1914 and was destined to gain a knighthood and become chairman of the Hawker Siddeley Group in 1963.

Expanding air force

The RAF's Expansion Scheme of the mid-to-late 1930s was destined to bring great prosperity to the aircraft industry, including Avro, which received an order for 287 Hawker Audax two-seat light bombers in 1935. By this time, the long and highly successful story of the Anson had already begun and would not come to an end until 15 May 1952, when the last of the 11,020 made left the factory at Yeadon.

With the clouds of war gathering over Europe again, the government sponsored a large number of aircraft factories across the country. Avro's involvement in this expansion began in August 1938, when Air Minister Sir Kingsley Wood flew into Woodford to visit the works at Newton Heath. Greeted by Roy Dobson, then the general manager of Avro, the air minister announced that a new factory was to be built on land located at Greengate, Chadderton.

Work on the new factory began immediately; a sense of urgency saw the building nearing completion by early 1939 and staff from Newton Heath were already making themselves at home from March. With no landing ground of its own, all aircraft constructed at Chadderton would be built in component form and transported to Woodford for final assembly and subsequent flight testing and delivery. As well as having a huge production line covering 750,000sq ft, the Chadderton plant would have one of the biggest aircraft design offices in the country, with 500 draughtsmen on the payroll at its peak.

The first aircraft to be built at Chadderton was the Bristol Blenheim, with a batch of Mk Is being delivered in August 1938. A total of 1,005 Blenheims, the bulk of them Mk IVs, were built by Avro at Chadderton, Newton Heath and Ivy Mill, Pailsworth, right up to October 1941; each and every one of them became a familiar site around Manchester as they were transported to Woodford for flight testing.

A new heavy bomber

While the Anson production line at Chadderton also gained momentum, Avro focused its attention on a specification for a new, advanced twin-engined bomber. First designed in 1937, the Manchester made its maiden flight at Ringway on 25 July 1939, and all looked rosy when an order for 200 aircraft was received from the Air Ministry. The Manchester was highly advanced for the time and its crew positioning, bomb load arrangement and defensive armament, not to mention the aircraft's systems, were state-of-the-art. However, the Manchester's Achilles' heel was the complex Rolls-Royce Vulture engines, which were far from ready to enter operational service. Considerably more Manchesters were lost through engine failures than enemy action, but out of the disappointment came inspiration, when Roy Chadwick rapidly returned to the drawing board.

The Manchester was redesigned to accommodate four Merlin engines, and, within a short space of time, one airframe was modified and in the air from Ringway on 9 January 1941; the Lancaster was born. Initial flight trials were successful, and within weeks, the plan to have Avro building Halifax bombers instead of the Manchester were scrapped in favour of mass-produced Lancasters.

The first of many Lancaster descendants appeared in 1942, when an experimental transport version named the York was created at Chadderton's Experimental Department. Within six months, the prototype was in the air, but focus on building the bombers had to be maintained, and full production of the York did not begin until almost at the war's end.

Sir Roy Dobson hands over the 11,020th and last Anson built, T Mk 21 WJ561, to the RAF on 27 May 1952. (*Aeroplane*)

Non-Avro military aircraft production

287 **Hawker Audax**: K5120 to K5176 (delivered between February and June 1936 to Contract 389427/35); K5561 to K5603 (delivered between April 1936 and April 1937 to Contract 458948/35 & 456498/35); and K8311 to K8335 ([India] delivered between March and June 1937 to Contract 401786/35).

1,005 **Bristol Blenheim**: L6594 to L6843 ([**Mk I**] delivered between August 1938 and March 1940 to Contract 588371/36); N3522 to N3545, N3551 to N3575, N3578 to N3604, N3608 to N3631 ([**Mk IV**] delivered between March and June 1940 to Contract 588371/36); R2770 to R2799 (delivered in June and July 1940 to Contract 588371/36); Z5721 to Z5770, Z5794 to Z5818, Z5860 to Z5909, Z5947 to Z5991, Z6021 to Z6050, Z6070 to Z6104, Z6144 to Z6193, Z6239 to Z6283, Z6333 to Z6382, Z6416 to Z6455 ([**Mk IV**] delivered between July 1940 to May 1941 to Contract B119994/40); Z9533 to Z9552, Z9572 to Z9621, Z9647 to Z9681, Z9706 to Z9755, Z9792 to Z9836 ([**Mk IV**] delivered between May and October 1941 to Contract B119994/40); and AE449 to AE453 ([**Mk IV**] Contract B1485/40, no evidence of delivery or service).

Two **Hawker Tornado** prototypes: R7936 (delivered July 1941 to Contract 12148/39).

75 **English Electric Canberra B Mk 2**: WJ971 to WJ995, WK102 to WK146 and WK161 to WK165 (delivered between April 1953 and March 1955 to Contract 6/Acft/5990).

Chadderton expansion

From early 1943, the Chadderton factory was expanded to over 1,000,000 sq ft of floor space, enabling Avro to raise productivity to 150 Lancasters per month (peaking at 155 in August 1944). Other impressive Chadderton figures included a wartime labour force that peaked at 11,267: out of this number, 7,887 worked on the day shift and 3,380 at night; 40.7 per cent of the labour was semi-skilled and 22.2 per cent were women.

Woodford also went through a period of expansion, the original aerodrome gaining several large flight sheds and, on the north side of the airfield, much larger assembly, and later production, facilities transformed this once quiet grass airfield. To help cope with Lancaster production, a 'shadow' factory was also established at Yeadon near Leeds (Leeds Bradford Airport today). Both Lancaster and Anson production were allocated to Yeadon, the latter reaching a peak production of 130 aircraft per month during 1943 and 1944.

At Chadderton, Chadwick set to work on an improved version of the Lancaster, designed for long-range operations in the Pacific theatre against the Japanese, named the Lincoln. An excellent aircraft in its own right, the Lincoln never had a chance to prove itself because the war ended before the bomber entered operational service. Large advanced production orders were reduced but the type still entered RAF service, bridging the gap between the multi-engine piston bomber and arrival of the jet-powered aircraft.

Chadwick's legacy

Sadly, Roy Chadwick was killed in a Tudor airliner on 23 August 1947, and was destined never to see the final two military designs he instigated take to the air. Both aircraft would serve the RAF for decades, beginning with a development of the projected anti-submarine Lincoln Mk III. The Shackleton, in its final guise as the AEW.2, was remarkably not retired until 1991, and in its

Maritime Reconnaissance role roamed the seas until replaced by the Nimrod in the early 1970s. The other design Chadwick launched was as far from the normal Avro style as possible but under the skin was a conventional machine. The breath-taking delta-winged Vulcan was also a long-serving aircraft, which remained in the RAF's front line until the early 1980s, when it was replaced by the highly capable Tornado, which was retired in 2019.

The 1950s saw a diverse range of Avro military aircraft leave the production lines, including the Athena trainer, the Ashton high-altitude research aircraft and the Avro 707 development aircraft in support of the Vulcan. At Chadderton, production also included a batch of 75 Canberra B.2 jet-bombers, which were delivered between April 1953 and March 1955. By the late 1950s, aircraft production began to slow and Avro was reduced to the Chadderton and Woodford sites only.

Blue Steel

A prediction in a memorandum issued by the Ministry of Supply in November 1954 stated that, by 1960, Soviet air defences would be efficient enough to make it impossible for a V-bomber to deliver a traditional gravity nuclear bomb. The solution to keeping the V-bombers out of harm's way was to launch the weapon at least 50 miles away from the target. This would mean an independent powerplant for a missile powerful enough to carry the device at supersonic speed. The device was designed to be carried by the Vulcan, Valiant and Victor and under the Air Staff Requirement OR.1132, issued in September 1954, it also had to be capable of Mach 3 and carry a Green Bamboo or Orange Herald nuclear warhead.

Despite having no previous experience of working on guided missiles, the contract to design and build the new weapon, named Blue Steel, was awarded to Avro. The work would be sensitive, so within the Chadderton site, a new high-walled compound was constructed with its own secure controlled entry.

Work commenced on Blue Steel in 1955; the guidance system being produced by Elliot Brothers, while the liquid fuel for the engine was developed by Armstrong Siddeley. A lack of knowledge of the size and weight of the proposed nuclear warhead caused a number of development problems and in the

The staff of *Aeroplane* was given access to the Chadderton factory in August 1942, where production of the Lancaster was already in full swing. These nose sections will be transported by road to Woodford where final assembly will take place. (*Aeroplane*)

Inside the massive final assembly shed at Woodford in June 1942, a scene that continued until the end of World War Two. (Via *Aeroplane*)

end, none of the British-designed warheads were used; instead, the US W.28 Red Snow thermonuclear warhead was employed. Once in service, the Blue Steel's inertial navigation unit was more advanced than the system carried in the actual bomber and, to take advantage of this, the crews would tie their own equipment into the missile's guidance system to plot the flight plan.

Blue Steel was large; it was 35ft 1in long, 48in in diameter and weighed 17,000lb. Power was provided by a twin-chamber Armstrong Siddeley Stentor Mk 101 rocket engine, which was fuelled by hydrogen peroxide/kerosene mix. Once launched, the Stentor engine produced 24,000lb of thrust that would propel Blue Steel at Mach 1.5, but as the target approached, a second 6,000lb chamber would be ignited, accelerating the missile to Mach 3 before the engine was cut and the weapon would free-fall drop and air burst.

Trials began at Woomera in Australia in 1960 and, in February 1963, the weapon finally entered service, by which time the V-force was reduced to the Vulcan and Victor. Prior to its entry into RAF service, more suitable weapons were sought because Blue Steel still lacked the range required to keep the bomber away from surface-to-air missiles. Development of the Blue Steel Mk 2 was scrubbed in 1960 so as not to delay the original weapon and the longer-range American-built AGM-48 Skybolt, which appeared to be ideal, was cancelled in 1962.

Each Blue Steel needed seven hours to prepare it for launch, and even then, it was doubtful whether the rocket engine would fire at the crucial moment. RAF estimates stated that at least half of the missiles would fail to fire and, defeating the whole object of the project, would have to be dropped in a free-fall manner over the target instead. The only short-term solution to outwitting the enemy's defences was to attack at low-level, under the radar. All Blue Steels in service were modified for a low-level launch but their usefulness in the event of a war was deemed as limited.

Avro produced 48 'live' Blue Steels, five more as spares and a further 20 non-nuclear rounds, 16 of which were used for training. Supplemented by 1,000lb WE.177 tactical and strategic nuclear bombs, Blue Steel remained in service until December 1970, when Britain's strategic nuclear capacity was transferred to the Royal Navy and its Polaris submarines.

Hawker Siddeley Aviation Limited

On 1 July 1963, Hawker Siddeley Aviation Limited (HSA) was created when Avro, Armstrong Whitworth and Hawker were amalgamated. The Avro 748 was already filling the Chadderton production lines, and overnight, the aircraft was redesignated as the HS.748. All the Avro expertise and

An example of production overlap at Woodford, with Lancaster Mk VIIs (B.7) approaching completion at the rear of the shed and the new Shackleton MR Mk 1 in the foreground. (*Aeroplane*)

A Vulcan bomber provides scale to the 35ft 1in-long Blue Steel rocket-assisted stand-off nuclear weapon. Despite being in RAF service from 1963 to 1970, the costly weapon never fully achieved its operational potential. (*Aeroplane*)

One of 75 Canberra B.2 bombers built by Avro in the mid-1950s, WK163 gained the World Altitude Record at 70,310ft in August 1957. (Via Martyn Chorlton)

Inset: One of two Roe blue plaques (the other is at Walthamstow) mounted on the wall of Brownsfield Mill, Binns Place, Ancoats, Manchester (the first workshop), which fittingly celebrates both Alliott and Humphrey. (Martyn Chorlton)

skilled workforce continued to serve HSA at both Chadderton and Woodford. Chadderton's designers were instrumental in producing the HS.801, aka the Nimrod, which would be built at Woodford.

Avro-built Shackletons and Vulcans would return to Woodford for modifications, upgrades and general servicing right up to the 1980s, while the 748 remained in production until 1989. A further overhauling of the aviation industry saw HSA disappear in 1977 to become British Aerospace (BAe), which in turn, was renamed again, in 1999, to the current BAE Systems. In the meantime, Chadderton was working on Airbus wings, components for the Advanced Turboprop (ATP) and the BAe 146, while Woodford provided Nimrod support and a variety of modifications for the RAF throughout the 1980s, 1990s and into the 21st century. Sadly, with the cancellation of the Nimrod MRA.4, the factory at Woodford and the airfield were closed down in 2011. Chadderton followed suit in early 2012, and the workforce was transferred to Samlesbury, which, along with Warton, are the last bastions of military aviation in Lancashire.

Avro as a historic name will hopefully live on while excellent facilities such as the Avro Heritage Centre at Woodford still exist. Despite plans to level Woodford and turn it into a combined housing estate and light industrial area, the heritage centre has its future secured so that generations to come can see for themselves the influence Avro had on this country's military aircraft during the 20th century.

An impressive view of the Vulcan production line at Chadderton in the 1950s. These giant components were all transported by road to Woodford for assembly. (*Aeroplane*)

500 & 502 (Type Es)

Development

The important step in the history of Avro's military aircraft began in response to the very first War Office aircraft specification, which was issued in 1911. The specification was quite demanding for the time and included the ability to carry a 350lb load (plus equipment), an endurance of 4½hrs and the capability of being delivered to Salisbury Plain in a crate.

Design

While very similar to the Duigan biplane designed the previous year, the Type E biplane differed by being larger and more powerful thanks to a 60hp E.N.V. water-cooled engine, which was mounted on the upper longerons of the fuselage. The E.N.V. was cooled by a pair of spiral tube radiators mounted either side of the fuselage for the prototype, but this layout was cleaned up for later aircraft. Although basic in every way, the general configuration of the Type E was revolutionary, and virtually all practical aircraft for the next two decades would follow the lead of the Avro machine.

The fuselage was made up by a box-girder construction of square section covered in fabric behind the powerplant and metal clad around the engine. The mainplanes were made up with ash spars, and each could be broken down in three sections to aid transportation by road.

Service

The Type E undertook its maiden flight on 3 March 1912 in the hands of Wilfred Parke from Brooklands. Named after the novelist Elinor Glyn, the Type E demonstrated a rare quality from the outset by actually having a reserve of power in hand. However, A. V. Roe was not entirely happy with it, and a second aircraft was fitted with a 50hp Gnome rotary. This aircraft performed even better, reaching a height of 2,000ft in just five minutes. On 9 May 1912, the aircraft was flown by Parke the 17 miles to Laffan's Plain in just 20 minutes, where it was demonstrated that afternoon in front of an appreciative official audience.

The second aircraft was officially designated as the Type 500, and in March 1912, a War Office contract ordered three machines, which were delivered to Farnborough and the Central Flying School (CFS) during May and June 1912. An order for four more followed for the RFC and the Admiralty ordered a pair as well; the latter order being delivered to Eastchurch in May 1913 and February 1914. A final batch, designated the Type 502, was delivered to Netheravon between March 1913 and January 1914. Examples saw service with 3 Squadron (May to August 1912), 5 Squadron (July 1913 to July 1914) and 7 Squadron (September 1914 and April 1915).

Production

Twelve Avro 500s were built to three military contracts, plus three individual builds. These were War Office Contract dated March 1912 for three aircraft, serialled 404–406; War Office Contract dated December 1912 for four aircraft, serialled 430, 432, 433 and 488, followed by an Admiralty Contract in 1913 for two aircraft serialled 41 and 150. One 500 was sold to the Portuguese government in October 1912, and two private sales were made before the outbreak of World War One, but both were later pressed into service as 939 with the RNAS and 491 with the RFC. Five Avro 502s were built under a single War Office Contract signed in January 1913; these were 285 and 288–291.

Technical data – Type E prototype & Avro 500	
ENGINE	(E) One 60hp E.N.V. Type F or 60hp A.B.C.; (500) One 50hp Gnome or 100hp Gnome
WINGSPAN	36ft
LENGTH	(E) 30ft 6in; (500) 29ft
HEIGHT	9ft 9in
WING AREA	330 sq ft
TARE WEIGHT	(E) 1,100lb; (500) 900lb
ALL-UP WEIGHT	(E) 1,650lb; (500) 1,300lb
MAX SPEED	(E) 50mph; (500) 61mph
INITIAL CLIMB RATE	(E) 170ft/min; (500) 440ft/min
ENDURANCE	(E) 6hrs

The first of just 12 Avro 500s that was flown from Brooklands on 8 May 1912 and delivered to Farnborough the following day. (Martyn Chorlton)

501 & 503 (Type H)

Development

By 1912, Avro was increasingly becoming interested in seaplanes, which timed well with the company's departure from Brooklands to Shoreham. Its first seaplane was a development of the Avro 500.

Design

The Avro 501, which on the surface looked like a bigger version of the 500 with floats, was built at Brownsfield Mills in November 1912. Powered by a 100hp Gnome, the aircraft first flew as an amphibian complete with a Gnosspelius-designed 15ft-long, 7ft-wide sprung central float that had three small wheels projecting slightly below it. The 47ft 6in-span aircraft was assisted on the water by a pair of wing tip floats, but the configuration proved to be unsatisfactory, and Gnosspelius replaced the single float with a more conformist twin-float arrangement.

The Avro 503, or Type H, was an even larger but more capable aircraft, which was constructed in sections so that it could be dismantled quickly for overland transportation.

Service

First testing of the Avro 501 took place on Lake Windermere in January 1913, followed by the Type H's maiden flight on 28 May 1913. The latter was conducted by F. P. Raynham, who was so confident in the aircraft he had one passenger on board (John Alcock, later of Atlantic crossing fame), two hours' worth of fuel and an anchor! Taking off after a run of just 60 yards, the aircraft handled well, and, later, having flown the Inspector of Naval Aircraft, Lt J. W. Seddon RN, an order for three aircraft was placed for the RNAS.

The German Navy also showed an interest in the Type H; Capt Schultz, a German naval officer, visited the Avro works several times while the prototype was being built. The Germans were so impressed they bought the Type H, and, after delivery to Wilhelmshaven on 3 September 1913, the aircraft was flown the 40 miles across the North Sea to the Island of Heligoland by Lt W. Langfeld and then onto Cuxhaven on 15 September. Peru also ordered a 503 Seaplane, but the outbreak of World War One prevented the deal from going ahead.

The original 501 was accepted by the RNAS as a landplane, the aircraft's structure being seen as so delicate that it earned the nickname 'Rickety Ann'. The first of the three 503s was delivered to the Isle of Grain in crates on 8 September1913. Having passed the RNAS trials with ease, all three aircraft were in service by October 1913, and No. 52 remained in use until January 1916.

Production

One Avro 501 seaplane was built, later converted to a landplane and serialled 16; this was followed by four Avro 503s. This batch consisted of the prototype, which was delivered to the German Navy as D12 and three aircraft for the RNAS, serialled 51–53.

Technical data – Avro 501 and 503 Seaplane	
ENGINE	One 100hp Gnome
WINGSPAN (Upper)	(501) 47ft 6in; (503) 50ft
WINGSPAN (Lower)	(501) 39ft 6in; (503) 47ft
LENGTH	(501) 33ft; (503) 33ft 6in
HEIGHT	(501) 12ft 6in; (503) 12ft 9in
WING AREA	(501) 478 sq ft; (503) 567 sq ft
TARE WEIGHT	(501) 1,740lb
ALL-UP WEIGHT	(501) 2,700lb; (503) 2,200lb
MAX SPEED	(501) 55mph; (503) 50mph
INITIAL CLIMB RATE	(503) 225ft/min

Avro 503 No. 52 at Chingford in 1915 – this was the second of just three aircraft originally built for the Royal Naval Air Service (RNAS) in seaplane form, but, as can be seen here, the machine has been converted into a landplane. (Martyn Chorlton)

504 & 504A to H

Development

The Avro 504 is one of the world's great iconic aircraft, and it firmly put A. V. Roe and his fledgling company on the aviation map. The Avro 504 caused quite a stir when it was revealed to the general public for the first time on 20 September 1913 at that year's Aerial Derby at Hendon. Not only did the 504 look fast, the aircraft went on to finish in fourth place, having achieved an average speed of 66.5mph. What is remarkable about this result is that the machine had only flown for the first time just two days earlier!

The first of a large number of War Office contracts was placed in 1913 for a dozen machines, followed by a tentative order by the Admiralty and a subsequent larger order for 44 aircraft, serialled 750 to 793, which would be the first to serve with the RFC. Who would have predicted then that the 504 would remain in production for almost two decades? Production finally came to an end in 1932, with just over 10,000 built, but it was World War One that saw the greatest demand, with 8,970 of those being constructed during the conflict.

Design

Being very similar in design to the Avro 500, work on the 504 began at Brownsfield Mills in November 1912. The first aircraft was completed at the Clifton Street works by early 1913. The design of the 504 was the responsibility of Chadwick and Taylor, who produced the fuselage and undercarriage, while H. E. Broadsmith focused on the wings.

The 504A was a strengthened version of the 504, with wide chord interplane struts and shorter ailerons. The 504B, which served with the RNAS, featured a larger fin, while the 504C was the single-seat anti-Zeppelin variant with additional fuel rather than an observer. The 504D was also a single-seat variant for the RFC, while the 504E featured a 100hp Gnome engine, the 504F a 75hp Rolls-Royce Hawk and the 504G an 80hp Gnome. The sole 504H was a modified 504C used for catapult trials under the watchful eye of Sqn Cdr E. H. Dunning.

Service

By the beginning of the war, large numbers of 504s were already in service, and as result, the first benchmark operations and victories were conducted by the Avro biplane. On 23 August 1914, Lt C. W. Wilson and his observer Lt C. E. C. Rabagliati forced down a Taube with a pistol, marking the first victory in action of the RFC. In the hands of the RNAS, three 504s successfully bombed the Zeppelin works at Friedrichshafen on 21 November 1914 using four 20lb bombs apiece.

It was not long before the 504 was obsolete over the trenches, but a new operational role as a Home Defence fighter to replace the B.E.2c saw the type remain operational until the end of the war. However, it was in the training role that the 504 excelled, and it was not long before it became the standard training machine for the RFC, RNAS and later the RAF during the post-war period.

Technical data – Avro 504A to H	
ENGINE	(Prototype) One 80hp Gnome or 80hp Monosoupape; (504 & 504A) One 80hp Gnome, 80hp Le Rhône, 80hp Clerget or 100hp A.B.C.; (504B) One 80hp Gnome or 80hp Le Rhône; (504C & 504D) One 80hp Gnome; (504E) One 100hp Gnome Monosoupape; (504F) 75hp Rolls-Royce Hawk; (504G & 504H) One 80hp Gnome
WINGSPAN	36ft
LENGTH	29ft 5in
HEIGHT	10ft 5in
WING AREA	330 sq ft
TARE WEIGHT	(504 land) 924lb; (504 sea) 1,070lb; (504A Le Rhône) 1,050lb
ALL-UP WEIGHT	(Prototype) 1,550lb; (504 land) 1,574lb; (504 sea) 1,719lb; (504A Le Rhône) 1,700lb
MAX SPEED	(Prototype) 81mph; (504 land) 82mph; (504 sea) 75mph; (504A Le Rhône) 86mph
CLIMB TO 3,000ft	(Prototype) 7mins
ENDURANCE	(Prototype) 3hrs; (504A Le Rhône) 4½hrs; (504C & D) 8hrs

Right: The first major War Office order for the Army was a batch of 44 Avro 504s, serialled 750 to 793, including No. 785. (Martyn Chorlton)

Below: The single seat of this 504 gives it away as an anti-Zeppelin 504C, shown here during service with the RNAS at Redcar. (Martyn Chorlton)

508

Development

Intended as a two-seat reconnaissance biplane for the RFC, the aircraft was never adopted for service, and instead the sole example ended its days in early 1916 as a flying school machine.

Design

The Avro 508 was a pusher biplane with twin-booms, which was the general layout of many aircraft at the time. Of wooden construction, the 508 was fabric-covered; its mainplanes were equal span, their design being very similar to the 504 prototype. The centre was quite wide-ending at the first of two pairs of interplane struts, the rear ones carrying the booms. Fitted with ailerons, the 508 broke new ground by being the first Avro machine to be fitted with aileron cables located within the wing. The cable ran along the inside of the leading edge, via internal pulleys.

The two crew were accommodated in tandem within a spacious nacelle, which was constructed from four ash longerons and crosscuts made of spruce. The pilot sat to the rear of the nacelle while the observer/air gunner was afforded excellent visibility by sitting in the nose of the aircraft.

Power was provided by an 80hp Gnome rotary engine, which was mounted on steel-tube bearers and was fed oil and fuel from tanks mounted immediately behind the pilot. The tail booms were also made of steel tube that was braced with spruce struts leading rearwards to the tailplane.

Service

The sole aircraft was built in December 1914 and during the following month was transported to Brooklands, where it was erected and flight tested. From a very early stage, the type appears to have been rejected by the RFC, but this did not stop Avro from displaying the 508 at the Belle Vue Gardens exhibition in Manchester from 1–3 January 1914. The aircraft was displayed without any fabric covering, but at a second and final public appearance at the Olympia Aero Show in London from 16–25 March 1914, the 508 was presented with covering.

The remainder of 1914 appears to have been quiet for the 508, which was not recorded again until April 1915 when it was declared 'operational' at Brooklands. The aircraft was then sold to the Hall Flying School at Hendon, which flew the aircraft until at least early 1916, and the 508 was mentioned as being stored in a dismantled state without engine in April of that year. The flying school had plans to fit dual controls and use the 508 for instruction and to carry passengers, but neither came to fruition.

Technical data – Avro 508	
ENGINE	One 80hp Gnome
WINGSPAN	44ft
LENGTH	26ft 9in
WING AREA	468 sq ft
TARE WEIGHT	1,000lb
ALL-UP WEIGHT	1,680lb
MAX SPEED	65mph
ENDURANCE	4½hrs

A tantalising glimpse of the Avro 508 at the Olympia Aero Show in London during March 1914. (Martyn Chorlton)

510

Development
Originally designed for the 1914 Circuit of Britain air race that was ultimately cancelled because of the outbreak of World War One, the Avro 510 broke new ground for the company – especially with regard to float design, which was sadly unappreciated by the RNAS.

Design
The 510 was a large two-bay seaplane designed to carry two crew in tandem. It bore a passing resemblance to previous Avro aircraft by having a bigger version of the 504 rudder installed. The 63ft upper mainplane overhung the lower by over 12ft at each end, and power was provided by a 150hp Sunbeam Nubian eight-cylinder water cooled engine. The Nubian was cooled by a large radiator mounted in the nose of the prototype, prominently and vertically positioned above the engine in the military production machines.

The float undercarriage was mounted upon four steel struts, which were in turn fitted to a tubular steel, rectangular-shaped frame. On the corners of the frame were the attachment points for the two main floats. These floats were a 'back to the drawing board' design, which incorporated a prominent taper to the rear of a single step. Smaller outboard floats were positioned under the lower mainplane and a larger single float, complete with rudder, was mounted below the tail.

Service
Constructed at Manchester in July 1914, the seaplane was delivered by rail direct to Calshot to take part in that year's Circuit of Britain race. A. V. Roe also travelled down to Calshot by road, and after spending the night at Havant woke to the news that Britain had declared war on Germany. As a result, the race was cancelled, but the re-erection of the 510 continued regardless, and a few days later the seaplane completed its maiden flight. The 510 was reported to fly well, and the new float design performed better than expected; landings in particular were much smoother than the earlier pontoon-type floats with their flat stern sections.

Once flight trials had been completed, A. V. Roe was approached by Capt Arthur Longmore of the Admiralty, who purchased the 510 there and then by handing over a cheque. On top of that, Longmore ordered five more production aircraft incorporating several modifications stipulated by the Admiralty. These included a modified longer undercarriage with an extra strut and, much to A. V. Roe's chagrin, the modern floats were to be replaced by the older type pontoon floats. The tail of the RNAS machines was also different, having a fixed fin with a rounded leading-edge rudder.

The RNAS 510s were delivered between December 1914 and April 1915, but unfortunately failed to fulfil their acceptance tests because of poor performance. All but one were later returned to the Supermarine Works at Woolston for modification, but none were ever reaccepted by the RNAS.

Production
One prototype was built, followed by five production aircraft ordered by the Admiralty for contract CP 30654/14. These aircraft were serialled No. 130 to 134; 130 to 132 were delivered to Killingholme, while 133 and 134 were delivered to Dundee. Only No. 130, which was put through trials at Grain, was retained by the RNAS; the remainder were returned between 19 and 26 October 1915.

Technical data – Avro 510	
ENGINE	One 150hp Sunbeam Nubian
WINGSPAN	(upper) 63ft; (lower) 38ft
LENGTH	38ft
WING AREA	564 sq ft
TARE WEIGHT	2,080lb
ALL-UP WEIGHT	2,800lb
MAX SPEED	70mph
CRUISING SPEED	85mph at 2,000ft
CLIMB RATE	1,000ft in 4½mins
ENDURANCE	4½hrs

A blurred photograph of the Avro 510 prototype at Calshot in July 1914, prior to its maiden flight. The machine was later sold to the Admiralty and serialled as No. 881. (Martyn Chorlton)

527

Development

Basically a modified 504E, the Avro 527 was being constructed at Manchester by A. V. Roe at the same time as work was being undertaken on the 523 Pike.

Design

Designed in December 1915 at the Park Works, Newton Heath, the 527 was a reconnaissance fighter biplane built specifically for the use of the RFC and clearly had its roots in the 504. The aircraft was fitted with a central skid and a fin and rudder, both of which were standard RNAS requirements of the day. It was powered by a 150hp Sunbeam engine, which was fitted with prominent twin exhausts extending at a slight angle vertically so that they expended their fumes above the mainplane. Cooling was provided by a large radiator mounted between the upper fuselage and lower upper mainplane, which would have caused considerable forward vision problems for the pilot. The 36ft-span mainplanes of the 527 were the same as those fitted to the 504K, but a larger aircraft, designated as the 527A, was to have a span of 42ft.

The one and only Avro 527, possibly during trials at Farnborough in 1916, which proved to be unsuccessful. (Martyn Chorlton)

With a crew accommodated in tandem, the rear cockpit was equipped with a single .303in Lewis machine gun for self-defence.

Service

Flight trials of the 527 began at Farnborough in early 1916, but these proved to be unsuccessful. The climb rate, figures for which are unknown, was particularly poor despite the 150hp delivered by the engine. The Sunbeam engine was actually deemed too powerful for the airframe, which had not been strengthened from the original 504K design.

The single aircraft, which was built to Works Order No. 2100, never received a military serial, and nothing is known of the aircraft's fate following the Farnborough trials.

Technical data – Avro 527	
ENGINE	One 150hp Sunbeam
WINGSPAN	36ft; (proposed 527A) 42ft
MAX SPEED	99mph
ARMAMENT	One .303in Lewis machine gun

521

Development

The Avro 521 was an attempt to produce an aircraft that incorporated all the best design features from a range of 504 variants, but unfortunately produced a machine that was very unforgiving. The latter was a trait that did not sit well with the 521's intended role as a trainer.

Design

Design work began on the 521 in late 1915, and progress must have been swift to the flight stage because of the large number of 504 features. The aircraft's straight upper longerons gave the machine a 504 air, while the general tail arrangement, including the tail skid, was lifted from the 504A. The 504E contributed with cockpit positions and centre-section struts, while the V-strut undercarriage was taken from the 504G, and the aerodynamic headrest for the pilot was from the 519. The 504 also contributed the mainplanes, although these were extensively modified with a span of 30ft, and large sections were removed from the trailing edges to provide better visibility for the pilot. A traditional Avro engine cowling concealed a 110hp Clerget rotary.

Other planned 521 variants included the 521A, which featured 42ft-span, three-bay wings. One 521A was actually built but not flown, while the 521B, which was to be fitted with standard 36ft-span 504 wings, never left the drawing board.

Service

The prototype, serialled 1811 (believed to have been the Works Order number), undertook its maiden flight from Trafford Park in the hands of F. P. Raynham in January 1916. He was accompanied by H. E. Broadsmith, who, standing in the rear cockpit wielding a dummy machine-gun, was assessing the effect of drag. Longitudinally unstable, Raynham did not find the 521 particularly pleasant to fly, but regardless the aircraft was delivered to Farnborough in February 1916. The RFC at this stage appears to have had more faith in the aircraft, and 25 production machines were ordered.

It is not clear exactly when, but construction of the production order was stopped at an early stage because of the 521's instability problems, and none were delivered to the RFC. At least one aircraft, most likely 1811, did end up the hands of the CFS at Upavon in the summer of 1916. Here, the aircraft was flown by several distinguished pilots and was generally described as a 'beast to fly'. One alarming trait was the 521's ability to enter a spin with ease during a right-hand turn. On 16 September 1916, Lt W. H. Stuart Garnett of the CFS Testing Flight lost his life when the 521 entered a spin at 1,500ft; a height from which recovery was impossible.

Production

A single prototype, serialled 1811, was initially ordered, followed by a production order for 25 521s, serialled 7520 to 7544, under contract 87A 234. Very few, if any, of the production batch were believed to have been built.

Technical data – Avro 521	
ENGINE	One 110hp Clerget
WINGSPAN	30ft; (521A) 42ft
LENGTH	28ft 2in
HEIGHT	9ft 10in
WING AREA	266 sq ft
TARE WEIGHT	1,150lb
ALL-UP WEIGHT	1,995lb
MAX SPEED	94.6mph at sea level
CRUISING SPEED	85mph at 2,000ft
CLIMB RATE	6,000ft in 14 mins
ENDURANCE	4½hrs
ARMAMENT	One .303in Lewis machine gun

The prototype Avro 521 at Farnborough in January 1916. (Martyn Chorlton)

519, 519A & 522

Development
Constructed for the Admiralty during early 1916, the Avro 519 and its siblings, the 519A and 522, were evolved from the 510 seaplane. The big biplane bomber was not a success and the four examples that were built, despite extensive flight testing, were most likely scrapped by mid-1917.

Design
The Avro 519 was a single-seat biplane bomber that featured folding wings, a conventional central skid undercarriage and a big fin and rudder, both of which derived from the 504B, albeit with larger dimensions. Only two examples of the 519 were built, followed by a pair of two-seat 519As, which, apart from the additional cockpit, differed by having a more substantial V-strut undercarriage fitted without a central skid.

The first of two 519s was fitted with side-mounted radiators, while the second 519 and the first 519A had their radiators mounted behind and above the engine. The latter position obstructed the pilot's forward vision and induced a significant amount of drag that the aircraft could not afford as the rate of climb was already poor. An attempt to improve the overall performance of the type saw the fourth and final machine built with equal-span wings and designated as the Type 522 by Avro, but it officially remained a 519A.

Service
The first 519, serialled 8440, completed its maiden flight in April 1916 and during that year was recorded as being at Eastchurch for quite some time. The second 519 was serialled 8441, while the next two aircraft, ordered by the RFC, were serialled 1614 and 1615. The latter was sent from the Park Works in Manchester to Hamble on 1 November 1916, where it was readied for military acceptance by early December 1916. However, 1615, along with 8441 and 1614, remained at Hamble until April 1917 when they left for an unknown, but presumably military, destination.

It seems that the departure of these three aircraft came as something of a relief for Avro, as company records record their move as 'managing to get rid' of them.

Production
Four aircraft, two 519s, 8440 and 8441, were ordered for the RNAS, followed by one 519A (1614) and one 522 (1615) ordered for the RFC.

Technical data – Avro 519, 519A & 522	
ENGINE	(519) One 150hp Sunbeam Nubian; (519A & 522) One 225hp Sunbeam
WINGSPAN	(519 & A upper) 63ft; (519 & A lower) 38ft; (522 upper & lower) 43ft
LENGTH	(519 150hp Sunbeam) 32ft 9in
HEIGHT	11ft 8in
WING AREA	600 sq ft
ALL-UP WEIGHT	(519) 3,000lb
SPEED	(519) 75mph
CLIMB RATE	6,000ft in 30min

Serialled as 1614, this aircraft was first of a pair of two-seat Avro 519As, both powered by a single 225hp Sunbeam engine. (Martyn Chorlton)

The second Avro 519A was unofficially designated by Avro as the Type 522 because of the number of modifications undertaken. Serialled as 1615, the aircraft had equal-span wings and, like 1614, was evaluated for RFC service. (Martyn Chorlton)

523 Pike & 523A

Development

The first of many Avro aircraft to receive a name, the 523 Pike was also the first machine to be erected at Hamble, which, along with a mile-long piece of foreshore at Southampton Water, had been purchased by A. V. Roe in 1916. Despite no large orders being received, the 523 Pike was a very advanced design, incorporating a host of features that would be used for many years to come.

Design

The 523 Pike, a big three-bay biplane, was designed by Roy Chadwick as a short-range night bomber or long-range photographic reconnaissance aircraft. Power for the 523 was provided by a pair of opposite-handed Sunbeam engines driven by pusher propellers. One novel feature, designed by A. V. Roe, was the bomb stowage, which was internal and horizontally tiered.

The pilot had excellent forward vision due to his position in front of the mainplanes, while air gunners were located in the extreme nose and in the dorsal position aft of the mainplane; both were equipped with .303in Lewis machine guns and, in the case of the 523 Pike, the front gunner had a pair.

Service

Although built in Manchester, the 523 Pike was sent to Hamble in the late summer of 1916, but erection work did not begin until late October. The work was carried out over a 12-day period, which ended on 11 November 1916, and it is presumed that the maiden flight was undertaken not long after. During early flight testing, new wings were ordered by the Admiralty, which were delivered to Hamble on 22 January 1917, and following their fitment the 523 Pike was described as being a good performer, especially considering the lack of horsepower. However, by this stage of World War One, large contracts had already been signed by the Admiralty with Short Brothers for a RNAS bomber, and the RFC were only interested in the big Handley Page. Although ready in February 1917, the 523 Pike was not actually delivered to the RNAS at Eastchurch until 24 March 1917.

A second aircraft, unnamed and simply designated as the 523A, was constructed at Manchester and test flown from the beach at Southport Sands in August 1916. Powered by a pair of 150hp Green engines, the 523A was initially flown with a triple-fin arrangement complete with 504-style comma rudders. By early September, the aircraft was allocated to the RFC and serialled A316. Moved from Southport to Hamble on 11 September, the aircraft was refurbished following its exposure to the unforgiving elements of the Lancashire coast.

The 523A was also converted to a tractor configuration following the refurbishment and flew again in this guise in February 1917. Following extensive trials with both the RNAS and RFC, both aircraft were returned to the company to continue as experimental aircraft; both were still in service at Hamble in 1918.

A 523B and 523C were also designed on paper, with high-horsepower Sunbeam and Rolls-Royce engines, but the Admiralty ordered the Avro 529 instead.

Technical data – Avro 523 & 523A Pike	
ENGINE	(523) Two 160hp Sunbeam; (523A) Two 150hp Green
WINGSPAN	60ft
LENGTH	39ft 1in
HEIGHT	11ft 8in
WING AREA	815 sq ft
TARE WEIGHT	(523) 4,000lb
ALL-UP WEIGHT	(523) 6,064lb
MAX SPEED	(523) 97mph
CLIMB RATE	5,000ft in 9½mins
ENDURANCE	7hrs

Right: Staff at the Hamble Works smile for the camera in early 1917 in the first Avro 523 'The Pike', which, at this stage, would have been given Works Order number 2230. (Martyn Chorlton)

Below: Ordered to contract 87/A/329 in April 1916, the first of two Avro 523As was serialled A316, pictured here on Southport Sands in August 1916. The second aircraft, A317, was not built. (Martyn Chorlton)

504J, K & Mk II

Development

The most widely used variants of the Avro 504 family by a wide margin were the 504J and 504K. Both types formed the backbone of the fledgling RAF's training programme beyond the end of World War One; the 504J being retired in September 1921, while the 504K soldiered on into the late 1920s and was not declared obsolete until March 1933.

Design

Externally identical to the 504A, the 504J differed by its powerplant, which was a 100hp Gnome Monosoupape or an 80hp Le Rhône. Large numbers of 504As were converted to 504J standard, the first examples being delivered to the School of Special Flying at Gosport from July 1917.

The 504K (aka the 'Clerget Avro') was once again no different on the outside from the 504J and only varied by having an open-front cowling and different engine bearers, enabling the aircraft to accommodate a wide range of air-cooled radial engines. The 504K's 'universal mounting' could be fitted with ten different rotary engines, including the 110hp Le Rhône, 130hp Clerget or 100hp Gnome Monosoupape.

The 504K Mk II, introduced in 1924, was a hybrid machine that was made up of a 504K fuselage with a 504N undercarriage and mainplane. The idea was shelved, and only four aircraft were built, all ending up on the civilian register.

Service

The 504J was ordered in huge numbers, and it was this aircraft that laid the foundation blocks for the RAF's Flying Training School syllabus for the next 40 years. The 504K bathed in the glory of what the 504J achieved and was first introduced in 1918, going on to become the standard equipment at the Central Flying School (CFS) and 1, 2, 3, 4 and 5 Flying Training Schools (FTS) until the Avro 504N began to arrive in the late 1920s.

The 504K even filled an operational void when it was the main equipment of 25 Squadron, the only RAF fighter squadron in Britain between January and April 1920, pending the arrival of the Sopwith Snipe. The 504K also served with 24 Squadron and the founding auxiliary units, 600, 601, 602 and 603 squadrons and Fleet Air Arm (FAA) units at Netheravon and Leuchars. The night fighter version of the 504K with a single seat also served with 33, 75, 76, 77 and 90 (Home Defence) squadrons.

Production

The exact breakdown of how many of each variant was produced is a grey area, but overall production of the 504 family built during World War One was 8,340 aircraft; 3,696 of these were built by Avro and 4,644 by subcontractors. In total, 5,446 were delivered to the RFC and RAF; 4,771 of these were delivered to Training Units, 274 to Home Defence Units, nine to the Expeditionary Force in 1914 and 392 to the Middle East. Almost 3,000 504s were still on RAF strength at the end of the war, 2,267 of them were operating from flying schools and 200 were still being employed on Home Defence duties.

Technical data – Avro 504J & K	
ENGINE	(J) One 80hp Le Rhône or 100hp Gnome Monosoupape; (K) One 90hp RAF.1A or 100hp Gnome Monosoupape, 90hp Thulin, 100hp Curtiss K.6, 100hp Sunbeam Dyak, 110hp Le Rhône, 130hp Clerget, 150hp Bentley B.R.1, 170hp A.B.C. Wasp I or 220hp Hispano-Suiza
WINGSPAN	36ft
LENGTH	(Rotary) 29ft 5in; (Dyak) 28ft 11in
HEIGHT	10ft 5in
WING AREA	330 sq ft
TARE WEIGHT	(504K Le Rhône) 1,251lb
ALL-UP WEIGHT	(504K Le Rhône) 1,800lb
MAX SPEED	(504K Le Rhône) 95mph
CLIMB TO 8,000ft	(504K Le Rhône) 6½mins
SERVICE CEILING	(504K Le Rhône) 16,000ft
ENDURANCE	(504K Le Rhône) 3hrs

Right: The world's only original airworthy Avro 504K, captured many years ago displaying the fictitious serial E3404, belongs to the Shuttleworth Collection based at Old Warden in Bedfordshire. Restored back in 1955 by Avro apprentices, the aircraft, whose original serial is H5199, was built by London Aircraft Co. Ltd in 1918. (Martyn Chorlton)

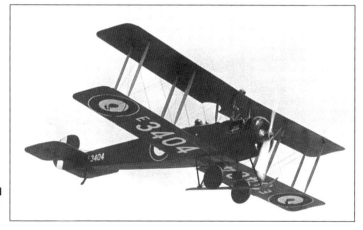

Below: Built from a batch of 150 aircraft ordered from Parnall & Sons Ltd, 504K F8748 first served with 1 Squadron RAF and then 5 FTS based at Sealand (aka Shotwick up to 1924). (Martyn Chorlton)

529 & 529A

Development

Even though the 523 Pike did not manage to secure the large bomber contracts on offer at the time, the Admiralty must have been interested in Avro's efforts because two bigger versions of the Pike designated the 529 and 529A were ordered in 1916 as long-range bombers.

Design

The 529s were large three-bay biplanes, complete with folding wings that bore many similarities to the Pike, and it was only the rudder shape that gave the new type away to the untrained eye. Power for the 529 was a pair of 190hp Rolls-Royce Falcon engines, which were uncowled and mounted mid-way between the two mainplanes, driving opposite handed propellers. The 529A differed in several different ways, including the engines, which were the more powerful 230hp B.H.P.s. These were fully cowled and mounted on the lower mainplane; the combined aerodynamic and increased power improvement meant that the maximum speed of the 529A was over 20mph faster. In fact, in all performance respects, the 529A beat the 529 hands down.

The two engine positions brought about two different fuel systems; in the case of the 529, fuel was carried in a 140-gallon tank in the centre of the fuselage, while the 529A had a 50-gallon tank mounted in each engine nacelle and a 10-gallon gravity tank above each powerplant.

Armament was provided by a pair of Scarff ring-mounted Lewis machine guns mounted in the nose and dorsal positions, and the rear gunner had a set of dual controls so that he could take over the aircraft in the event of an emergency. The front gunner also carried out the duties of the bomb aimer and communicated with the pilot via a Gosport tube. The 529A was capable of carrying up to 20 50lb bombs stowed vertically within the fuselage between the main spars of the lower mainplane.

Service

The 529, serialled 3694, was built in Manchester and assembled at Hamble, where it made its maiden flight in March 1917. The 529A, serialled 3695, was delivered to Hamble in a part-constructed state to make way for 504K production.

Both 529s were delivered to the Aeroplane and Armament Experimental Establishment (A&AEE) at Martlesham Heath for trials, the 529A arriving on 31 October 1917, only to crash on 11 November following a rudder failure. The latter problem had already occurred to the 529, which managed to land safely during its early flight trials in March 1917. The 529 later flew comparative trials with the Blackburn Kangaroo at Martlesham Heath in January 1918, and this was the last time the Avro bomber was heard of.

Both 529s suffered from poor elevator control, but the 529A in particular was a good overall performer taking in to account its combined 460hp and an ability to fly on one engine. However, no big production order came about, and only the two prototypes were ever built.

Production

Two prototype aircraft were ordered under contract CP 122495/16, designated Avro 529 and Avro 529A and given RFC serials 3694 and 3695, respectively.

Technical data – Avro 529 & 529A	
ENGINE	(529) Two 190hp Rolls-Royce Falcons; (529A) Two 230hp B.H.P.s
WINGSPAN	86ft 2in
LENGTH	64ft 7in
HEIGHT	17ft 5in
WING AREA	840 sq ft
EMPTY WEIGHT	18,000lb
GROSS WEIGHT	28,500lb
MAX SPEED	255 mph at 15,000ft
SERVICE CEILING	18,000ft
RANGE	2,200 miles with 1,500lb bomb load & 1,540 miles with a 4,500lb bomb load

Above: Avro 529A 3695 is fitted with a pair of 230hp Galloway-built B.H.P. engines, which were mounted within nacelles positioned on the lower mainplane. (Martyn Chorlton)

Right: Serialled 3694, the prototype Avro 529 was powered by a pair of uncowled Rolls-Royce Falcon engines that were mounted mid-gap between the mainplanes and drove a pair of opposite handed wooden four-bladed propellers. (Martyn Chorlton)

528 Silver King

Development
A derivative of the Avro 519, the 528 Silver King was first ordered by the Admiralty in September 1915 as a 'bomb dropper'. It was the intention of both Avro and the Admiralty to have the aircraft available for the forthcoming Admiralty competitive trials in March 1916. This proved to be unachievable, as only the drawings were ready by that date, and the aircraft itself would not be completed until September. Further problems and delays caused by manufacturing faults gave the aircraft no chance of receiving orders from the Admiralty, which washed its hands of the 528 Silver King by early 1917.

Design
The 528 Silver King was a large 65ft-span two-seat bomber, which was fitted with folding wings. Power was provided by a single 250hp Sunbeam engine cooled by a pair of large unsightly radiators mounted either side of the upper fuselage under the mainplane, which once again caused forward visibility problems for the pilot. Another feature was a pair of faired bomb racks mounted on each lower mainplane, just inboard of the point where the wing folded.

Service

The sole 528 Silver King was finally despatched from the Park Works in Manchester to Hamble on 9 September 1916. The troubled life of the aircraft continued as manufacturing faults were found within the structure, and these had to be rectified before re-erection could be carried out. The Sunbeam engine also caused problems and 528 Silver King did not re-emerge from the Hamble workshops until 19 December 1916.

Engine troubles continued to plague the aircraft, which were not cured even when the Sunbeam was replaced by a new unit. The problem was not perceived as being the propeller, but after several were tried, the 528 Silver King performed no better, and it may have come as some relief when the Admiralty announced that it would not accept the aircraft 'under any circumstances' on 24 February 1917.

Despite this decision, the Admiralty still thought the aircraft may be of some use as an experimental machine, but whether this was ever achieved is unknown, because the last sighting of the aircraft was at Hamble in April 1917.

Technical data – Avro 528	
ENGINE	One 250hp Sunbeam
WINGSPAN	(upper) 65ft; (lower) 55ft
LENGTH	33ft 8in
ALL-UP WEIGHT	5,509lb

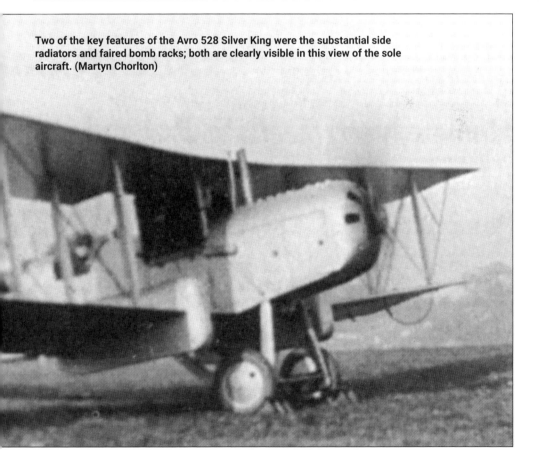

Two of the key features of the Avro 528 Silver King were the substantial side radiators and faired bomb racks; both are clearly visible in this view of the sole aircraft. (Martyn Chorlton)

530

Development

The Avro 530 was 'almost' one of the greatest aircraft of World War One, but it was let down by the non-availability of 300hp Hispano-Suiza water-cooled engine and had to make do with the 200hp version. Even with the latter engine, the Avro 530 performed as well as its main rival, the Bristol F.2a Fighter. However, when the 200hp Hispano-Suiza was diverted to SE.5a production, the Avro 530 was left high and dry and only a pair of prototypes was built.

Design

The Avro 530 was an aerodynamic, uncluttered design featuring a deep fuselage made up of a box-girder construction, wire-braced and fabric-covered. The Hispano-Suiza engine was mounted on duralumin girders and cooling was provided by a large frontal radiator. The aircraft was operated by a crew of two, the pilot, occupying the forward cockpit, had a single fixed-forward firing Vickers machine gun, while behind him, an observer/gunner was furnished with a Scarff ring mounted Lewis machine gun. Initially, the fixed Vickers was housed inside a large fairing, but as this obstructed the pilot's view to the front, the forward upper fuselage decking was reshaped and the fairing reduced in size.

Service

The first Avro 530, serialled B3952, was built in Manchester but re-erected at Hamble, where it was flown for the first time in July 1917. As mentioned, the aircraft was powered by a 200hp Hispano-Suiza and, despite the lack of horsepower, the aircraft performed well during manufacturer's trials, but little is known as to whether or to what degree the aircraft was evaluated by the RFC.

The second prototype, serialled B3953, went some way to make up the power deficiency as it was installed with a 200hp Sunbeam Arab engine when it was first flown in 1918. The aircraft was also modified with an unfaired, wide-angle 'V' undercarriage, a larger more attractive fin and the mainplane section was changed to an RAF 15, from the original aircraft's RAF 14 section.

There was no further interest from the military by this stage, as the Bristol F.2a and subsequent F.2b had already achieved large orders and development of the Avro 530 was ended. However, neither aircraft was scrapped by Avro, and at least one was used as a demonstrator in 1920 as a high-speed tourer. The aircraft's deep fuselage could be used to carry a large amount of baggage and the twin cockpits were demilitarised and made more comfortable for a civilian market. It is not clear if the modification work was ever carried out, or if a civilian serial was applied to either aircraft.

Production

Two prototypes were ordered under contract AS.425/17 on 15 May 1917 with serials B3952 and B3953. The serials B9431 and B9432 were set aside to the same contract on 26 July 1917 but not used.

Technical data – Avro 530	
ENGINE	(1st Proto) One 200hp Hispano-Suiza; (2nd Proto) One 200hp Sunbeam Arab
WINGSPAN	36ft
LENGTH	28ft 6in
HEIGHT	9ft 7in
WING AREA	325½ sq ft
TARE WEIGHT	1,695lb
ALL-UP WEIGHT	2,680lb
MAX SPEED	114mph
CRUISING SPEED	95mph
CLIMB RATE	5,000ft in 6mins 30secs
SERVICE CEILING	18,000ft
ENDURANCE	4hrs

The Avro 530 in its final form, complete with spinner, faired undercarriage, bigger fin and small centre-section fairing. (Martyn Chorlton)

531 Spider

Development
The 531 Spider was an unprompted design that Avro had clearly put great faith in being ordered in significant numbers to replace the single-seat 504K night fighters that were serving with Home Defence squadrons at the time.

Design
The private-venture Spider was a single-seat fighter that used a large number of 504K components to speed up the manufacture of the new aircraft. A conventionally built, shorter fuselage was joined to the forward fuselage of a 504K, while power was initially provided by an 110hp Le Rhône. Another practical feature of the little fighter was the rigging, which dispensed with the traditional wires and replaced them with steel Warren girder interplane struts/bracing. This was made up of six faired steel tubes, which were arranged in three upside-down triangles on each side. These were attached to the lower spar of the lower mainplane and the twin main spars of the upper mainplane. The lower wing of the Spider was much shorter than the upper and only had a chord of 2ft 6in.

The pilot enjoyed a good field of vision despite the upper mainplane being fitted so close to the top of the fuselage. This was achieved by cutting a large circular aperture in the upper mainplane, through which the pilot's head protruded. The Spider was armed with a single synchronised .303in Vickers, which was mounted slightly off-centre to starboard on top of the forward fuselage.

An extensively modified version of the Spider was designated as the 531A. This machine featured heavily staggered wire-braced mainplanes and 504K interplane struts. Power was provided by a 130hp Clerget and construction was believed to have begun in early 1919. The aircraft never came to fruition, but it is presumed that the 531A's major incomplete components were incorporated in the civilian Avro 538.

Service
First flown in April 1918, the Spider was an instant favourite with all who were lucky enough to fly it. The fighter handled beautifully, and with plenty of power in hand, the harmonised controls made the aircraft very manoeuvrable. During early flight trials, the Spider was further improved when a 130hp Clerget was fitted, and plans were also made to use a 150hp Bentley B.R.I and a 170hp A.B.C. Wasp I.

Between 27 April and 18 May 1918, the Spider was detached to the School of Special Flying at Gosport, and during this time, experienced pilots of the day were invited to fly the aircraft. The Spider returned to Gosport again on 13 July and continued to cause quite a stir with RFC pilots to such an extent that the Air Ministry could not fail to hear about the new Avro fighter.

Regardless of the enthusiasm being shown for the Spider, the Air Ministry had already selected the Sopwith Snipe as the RAF's new standard single-seat fighter. Only one Spider was destined to be built, and this remained in use as an experimental aircraft until at least the summer of 1919.

Technical data – Avro 531 Spider	
ENGINE	(531) One 110hp Le Rhône or 130hp Clerget; (531A) One 130hp Clerget
WINGSPAN	(531 upper) 28ft 6in; (531A upper) 28ft; (531 lower) 21ft 6in; (531A lower) 27ft
LENGTH	20ft 6in
HEIGHT	(531) 7ft 10in; (531A) 8ft 6in
WING AREA	(531) 189 sq ft
TARE WEIGHT	(531) 963lb; (531A) 960lb
ALL-UP WEIGHT	(531) 1,517lb; (531A) 1,514lb
MAX SPEED	120mph
CLIMB RATE	5,000ft in 4mins
SERVICE CEILING	19,000ft
ENDURANCE	(531A) 3hrs

Right: **The prototype Avro 531 Spider, which was powered by a 110hp Le Rhône rotary engine. (Martyn Chorlton)**

Below: **The Spider was described as a delight to fly, the controls were powerful and harmonised, making the little fighter extremely manoeuvrable. (Martyn Chorlton)**

533 Manchester
Mk I, II & III

Development

The 533 Manchester represented the finale for the Pike/529 series of aircraft and was designed to an Air Ministry specification that included a requirement for a pair of new 320hp A.B.C. Dragonfly I seven-cylinder radial engines. Despite the aircraft's name, the Manchester was constructed entirely at Hamble.

Design

The Manchester was a much more refined aircraft than its predecessors, beginning with the fuselage, which was much deeper, making life better for the crew. The tail unit was also improved with a design similar to that used by de Havilland many years later, while the ailerons were balanced with 'park-bench' aerofoils above the upper mainplane.

Completed by October 1918, the first Manchester was being prepared for covering when the original engine specification was changed to a pair of 300hp Siddeley Puma high-compression, water-cooled engines. This change was necessary because the Dragonfly engines were behind schedule, but, once the Puma engines were delivered in November 1918, the original aircraft was redesignated as the 533A Manchester Mk II.

The Dragonfly engines finally arrived in December 1918, and these were installed in the Manchester Mk I. Other than the engines, the Mk I and II only differed by their wing areas and slightly different tail units. Both aircraft shared a balanced rudder, but the surface area of the tail of the Mk I was greater than the Mk II. Another difference was an unbalanced elevator on the Mk I and a balanced one on the Mk II.

Service

The Manchester Mk II, serialled F3492, first flew in December 1918. On 20 December, the aircraft was delivered to 186 Development Squadron at Gosport until 9 January 1919 and then onto the A&AEE at Martlesham Heath in March 1919. F3492 remained at Martlesham until September 1919, and after returning to Hamble, Avro planned to re-engine the aircraft with Napier Lions, but this never came about.

The second aircraft, Manchester Mk I F3493, undertook protracted manufacturer's tests until October 1919, when it was delivered to Martlesham Heath. Both aircraft were reported as being good performers, especially considering how little power both Manchesters had to play with. Despite being a large aircraft, the Manchester could be easily looped and deliberately spun with little fuss during the recovery. However, the requirement for an aircraft of this type had already passed, and peacetime RAF needs did not include an aircraft like the Manchester and no production orders were forthcoming.

A third aircraft's airframe, the Manchester Mk III serialled F3494, reached an advanced stage, but the intended two 400hp Liberty 12 engines were never fitted.

Production

Two complete 533 Manchesters were built: one Mk I serialled F3493 and one Mk II serialled F3492. F3494 only reached the airframe stage.

Technical data – Manchester Mk I, II & III	
ENGINE	(Mk I) Two 320hp A.B.C. Dragonfly I; (Mk II) Two 300hp Siddeley Puma; (Mk III) Two 400hp Liberty 12
WINGSPAN	60ft
LENGTH	37ft
HEIGHT	12ft 6in
WING AREA	(Mk I) 813 sq ft; (Mk II) 817 sq ft
TARE WEIGHT	(Mk I) 4,887lb; (Mk II) 4,574lb
ALL-UP WEIGHT	(Mk I) 7,390lb; (Mk II) 7,158lb
MAX SPEED	(Mk I) 112mph; (Mk II) 119mph
CLIMB RATE	(Mk I) 10,000ft in 14mins 20secs; (Mk II) 10,000ft in 16mins 30secs
SERVICE CEILING	(Mk I) 19,000ft; (Mk II) 17,000ft
ENDURANCE	(Mk I) 5¾hrs; (Mk II) 3¾hrs

Avro 533 Manchester Mk I F3493 was actually the second of just two examples to fly and was powered by a pair of 320hp A.B.C. Dragonfly I engines. (Martyn Chorlton)

Avro 504K
(Foreign Air Forces)

Aircraft Disposal Co. Ltd (ADC)

During 1919 and 1920, an Imperial Gift of surplus Avro 504Ks was made by the British government to the Dominions. Over the following 12 years, huge numbers of 504Ks were stripped, overhauled and test flown by the Aircraft Disposal Co. Ltd at Croydon, from where aircraft were dispatched to air forces, navies and civilian operators across the world.

Service

Australia: Forty-eight Imperial Gift 504Ks were in service with the Australian Flying Corp by 1920, serialled A3-1 to A3-48. A large number of these aircraft were still in service until 1928, when they were replaced by the de Havilland Moth.

Belgium: Following a demonstration at Brussels in August 1920 by a pair of 504Ks, the Belgium government placed an order for 12 aircraft from Vickers Ltd, including six converted by Avro at Hamble. These were to re-equip the 8th Group of l'Aeronautique Militaire. A further 38 were purchased via the ADC, and additional aircraft for the Belgian Air Force were built under licence at Evère by SABCA. British-supplied 504Ks were serialled A1 to A50, while the SABCA-built machines were serialled A51 to A78.

Canada: Five hundred 504Ks were planned to be built by Canadian Aeroplanes Ltd in 1918, but only two had been constructed when the contract was cancelled. Post-war, 63 Imperial Gift 504KS were supplied to the Canadian Air Force from 1920, the majority of them serving at Camp Borden, where they were employed on pilots' refresher courses.

Denmark: Six 504Ks were purchased by the Danish government from the ADC for service with the Danish Navy, with the aircraft arriving on 29 December 1920. Two out of the six survived for conversion to 504Ns in 1928. The Danish aircraft were serialled 101 to 106. Two further aircraft were purchased for service with the Danish Army, serialled Avro 1 and Avro 2.

Finland: A single aircraft, 504K G-EBNU/E448, served with the Finnish Air Force after being purchased from the ADC in 1926. Serialled AV-57, the aircraft was retired in 1930.

Ireland: Five 504Ks were purchased from the ADC and Central Aircraft Co. for the Irish Air Corp in 1921. They were serialled I to V.

Japan: The Imperial Japanese Navy was initially equipped with 20 504Ks brought to the country by a British mission in April 1921. Subsequently, licensed production was undertaken by Nakajima at Ohta-Machi, but the majority of these were for the civilian market.

Mexico: 504Ks were built under licence at Balbuena for the Mexican Air Force to serve with the main flying school from 1922 to 1930.

Netherlands Indies: Between 1919 and 1922, the Netherlands Indies Army Air Force received 36 504Ks, supplemented by 16 more that were built locally at Andir in 1924. The aircraft were serialled A-21 to A-56 (British-built) and AL-57 to AL-73 (locally built). After being re-engined with the 130hp Mongoose, the type remained in service until 1933.

New Zealand: An air arm (later called the New Zealand Permanent Air Force [NZPAF]) was not formed in New Zealand until 1923. Several 504Ks that were originally supplied as Imperial Gifts in 1920 were inherited by the new air force.

Norway: A pair of ex-RFC 504As (serialled F-1 & F-7) were re-erected by the Norwegian Army Air Force in early 1918, followed by three 504Ks (serialled 103 to 105) bought from England in 1920.

Portugal: The Portuguese government bought 30 504Ks from Vickers Ltd in 1923 serialled 1 to 30. The type served with the Cintra Flying School from 1924 up to the late 1920s and four remained in service with the Grupo de Esquadrilhas de Aviação 'Republica' until 1934.

South Africa: Fifteen Imperial Gift 504Ks were supplied to the South African Air Force, the majority of them remaining in service until 1927 when they were replaced by the 504N in a host of roles.

South America: One 504K was gifted to Argentina in 1921 and a further nine were purchased for the country's main military flying school at El Palomar. The Brazilian Naval Air Service initially operated four 504Ks from 1920, which were joined by eight more in 1921. Chile flew ten reconditioned 504Ks from their main flying school at Lo Espejo from 1921, and the Guatemalan Air Force purchased several 504Ks in 1924. The Peruvian Air Force and Navy operated a number of 504Ks, and four were also operated by the Uruguayan Air Force from 1920.

Spain: A single 504K was maintained by the Spanish Air Force for the personal use of King Alphonso from mid-1919, and further aircraft were supplied to military flying schools. Four were purchased for the Spanish Royal Naval Air Service in 1925 and were flown from Barcelona.

Sweden: The Swedish Navy operated five 504Ks serialled 6 to 10 from 1923 until 1928.

Ex-H2023 was one of six 504Ks purchased from the Aircraft Disposal Co. Ltd for service with the Danish Navy from early 1921. No. 104 was one of two that survived to be converted to 504N standard and re-serialled as 112 in 1928. (Martyn Chorlton)

504L

Development

The 504L was the designation given to a seaplane version of the 504K, and the 'L' was more about the float undercarriage, which was produced in large numbers as a conversion kit. Not accepted by the RAF, the 504L sold in reasonable numbers on the civilian market and also served with several countries in a military training role.

Design

The first aircraft to be converted was C4329, which was originally built by Avro as a 504J. The aircraft was fitted with a pair of pontoon-type, single-step floats, which were attached to the fuselage by a pair of steel struts apiece. The 504L was also fitted with tail and wingtip floats, which were attached directly to the main structure. The fuselage was contoured better to blend in with the shape of the engine cowling, a modification that later featured on the 504N. Power was provided by a 130hp Clerget driving a two bladed propeller, which was replaced by a four-bladed unit not long after trials began.

Service

Manufacturer's trials began at Hamble in February 1919, but there was no interest in the aircraft as a training seaplane from the RAF or the Admiralty. The 504L did cause some interest on the civilian market, especially when higher-powered engine installations were offered. The Royal Australian Air Force (RAAF) operated two 504Ls, the RNZAF three examples, and at Valparaiso, the Chilean Air Force flew three 504L seaplane trainers with 130hp Clerget engines.

The largest military operator of the 504L was the Imperial Japanese Navy with ten aircraft on strength, which were part of a selection of machines that took part in a British mission led by Col the Master of Sempill in 1921. By September of that year, the British were training Navy pilots to fly the 504L from Kasumigaura near Tokyo, and, not long after, the Japanese government purchased the manufacturing rights of the aircraft, which were built by Nakajima with 150hp Bentley B.R.1 engines.

Production

Military 504Ls included C4329 (the 504J), followed by H2581, H2582, H2585, H2590 and H2589; these five aircraft were 504K conversions, which all sold on the civilian market by September 1919. Imperial Gift conversions were E361, H2041, H2044, H2045 and H9729 to Canada; H3034 (A3-46) and H3042 (A3-47) to the RAAF; H2986, H2988 and H2990 (G-NZAC) to the RNZAF. An unknown number of 504Ls were built by Nakajima, which commenced with serial J.N.752 from 1921 and were known to have reached R.603, R.604 and R.605 by 1926.

Technical data – Avro 504L	
ENGINE	One 110hp Le Rhône, 130hp Clerget or 150hp Bentley B.R.1
WINGSPAN	36ft
LENGTH	32ft 1in
HEIGHT	11ft 4in
WING AREA	330 sq ft
TARE WEIGHT	1,408lb
ALL-UP WEIGHT	2,006lb
MAX SPEED	87mph
CRUISING SPEED	75mph
INITIAL CLIMB RATE	650ft/min
ENDURANCE	2hrs

Originally built as a 504J by Avro, C4329 was converted into the prototype 504L in early 1919 and is seen here at Hamble during trials in February of that year. The aircraft has a four-bladed propeller and no wing-tip floats. (Martyn Chorlton)

504N

Development
Initial development of what would become the last variant of the highly successful 504 family began in 1919, riding on the back of what had been achieved in such a short space of time during World War One. Designed to replace the 504K, the 'N' gave excellent service with a host of RAF training units.

Design
Trials began using a 504K in 1919, with an A.B.C. Wasp I fitted, and continued into 1922 when two more 504Ks, E9265 and E9266, were trialled with a 150hp Armstrong Siddeley Lynx engine. Two official 504N prototypes followed, J733 being fitted with a Bristol Lucifer and J750 with an 180hp Lynx; both of these aircraft were fitted with a Siskin-type undercarriage.

Production 504Ns were fitted with oleo-pneumatic undercarriage, which could take a lot of punishment, twin fuel tanks under the upper mainplane and a more rounded fuselage thanks to extra stringers. Early 504Ns were fitted with wooden fuselages and tapered ailerons, while later production machines had fuselages made of welded steel tube and rectangular Frise ailerons.

Service
Production of the RAF's first new post-war trainer began in 1927 and continued until 1933. The 504N became the standard RAF trainer with all the major flying schools, including 1, 2, 3, 4 and 5 FTS. The type also served with the CFS at Wittering, where the school's 'E' Flight pioneered instrument flying in the RAF and began to train the art to students from September 1931. The six 504Ns that served with the flight were modified with blind-flying hoods, Reid and Sigrist turn indicators, and the wings were adjusted so that they had less dihedral to reduce the machines inherent stability.

The 504N also served as a communications aircraft with 24 Squadron, several auxiliary squadrons and the majority of University Air Squadrons into the 1930s before it was superseded by the Avro Tutor.

The 504N was not only remembered with affection by the hundreds of RAF pilots who learnt to fly in them, but also the general public who were lucky enough to enjoy the Hendon air displays between 1930 and 1933. The exhibitions of 'crazy flying' were hugely popular.

Production
There were 511 Avro 504Ns built in 11 production batches for the RAF and a further 78 were converted from 504Ks. The type also received orders from foreign customers including the Belgium Air Force, Brazilian Naval Air Service, Chilean Naval Air Service and Danish Navy. Five of the six aircraft that served with the Danish Navy were built in Denmark under licence and were designated as the L.B.1 (Land Biplane I).

Technical data – Avro 504N	
ENGINE	One 180hp Armstrong Siddeley Lynx IV or 215hp Lynx IVC
WINGSPAN	36ft
LENGTH	28ft 6in
HEIGHT	10ft 11in
WING AREA	320 sq ft
TARE WEIGHT	1,584lb
ALL-UP WEIGHT	2,240lb
MAX SPEED	100mph
CRUISING SPEED	85mph at 2,000ft
INITIAL CLIMB RATE	770ft/min
SERVICE CEILING	14,600ft
ENDURANCE	3hrs

Avro 504Ns K1049 and K1246 are in service with Cambridge University Air Squadron circa 1933. Both of these aircraft were later sold on the civilian market in 1934. (Martyn Chorlton)

555 Bison Mk I & 555A Bison Mk IA & II

Development

The Avro 555 Bison was a typical example of an aircraft built to the exact letter of the specification submitted. The specification in question – 3/21 (DoR Type 7A) – called for a sea reconnaissance and fleet gunnery spotting biplane, capable of operating from an aircraft carrier. As with all naval requirements, the practicality and functionality of the aircraft came a long way ahead of pleasing looks.

Design

The Bison was an extremely unattractive aircraft, beginning with a sloping nose, which was required because of the high position of the pilot's cockpit, in front of the upper mainplane, to aide carrier landings. Buried underneath the sloping engine cowling was a 450hp Napier Lion water-cooled engine, which sat on a special mounting that doubled as a maintenance work stand whilst the powerplant was removed.

The tubular steel fuselage was covered by plywood in the centre section to form a cabin with big observation windows on either side, together with a pair of forward port holes. The cabin was spacious enough for radio and navigation equipment, a plotting table, and the crew even had enough headroom to stand up. A gunner's position was accessed from the rear of the cabin; this was armed with a Scarff ring-mounted Lewis, while the pilot had a fixed-forward firing Vickers machine gun. The mainplanes were of a high-lift design and could be folded when the aircraft was stowed below decks. The aircraft was also fitted with a set of floatation bags mounted in the front and rear of the fuselage, so that it would float in the event of a ditching at sea.

Production aircraft fitted with a four-bladed propeller were designated as the Mk IA, while later machines were referred to as the Mk II. The latter had no forward port holes, a big centre-section and an undercarriage without arrestor claws.

Technical data – 555 Bison Mk I & Mk II	
ENGINE	One 480hp Napier Lion II
WINGSPAN	46ft
LENGTH	36ft
HEIGHT	(Mk I) 13ft 6in; (Mk II) 14ft 2in
WING AREA	(Mk I) 620 sq ft; (Mk II) 630 sq ft
TARE WEIGHT	(Mk I) 4,160lb; (Mk II) 4,116lb
ALL-UP WEIGHT	(Mk I) 5,800lb; (Mk II) 6,132lb
MAX SPEED	(Mk I) 110mph; (Mk II) 108mph
CRUISING SPEED	90mph
INITIAL CLIMB RATE	(Mk I) 600ft/min; (Mk II) 450ft/min
SERVICE CEILING	(Mk I) 14,000ft; (Mk II) 12,000ft
RANGE	(Mk I) 340 miles; (Mk II) 360 miles

Service

The prototype Bison, serialled N153, made its maiden flight in June 1922, followed by two modified prototypes in October and December. It was first trialled by the A&AEE at Martlesham Heath in August 1922 and the RAF base at Gosport, where it was the intention to re-equip 3 Squadron from the Walrus to the Bison. However, 3 Squadron disbanded on 1 April 1923, before the Bison arrived and was split into 420, 421 and 422 flights. Subsequently, all of the first 12 production Bison Mk Is were diverted to 423 Flight operating from HMS *Argus* from November 1923.

From early 1925, 423 Flight began to re-equip with the Bison Mk II followed by 421, 421A, 421B, 447 and 448 flights, which between them also operated from HMS *Eagle*, *Furious*, *Glorious* and *Hermes*, until 1929, when the type was superseded by the Fairey IIIF.

Production

Three prototypes, N153 to N155, followed by an initial production batch of 12 Bison Mk I built at Manchester to Air Ministry order 1922, serialled N9561 to N9602. Also built at Manchester were 41 Bison Mk IIs, divided into four batches; 18 aircraft serialled N9836 to N9853, ordered in July 1924; 12 aircraft serialled N9966 to N9977, ordered in December 1924; six aircraft serialled S1109 to S1114, ordered in November 1926; and five aircraft serialled S1163 to S1167, ordered in February 1927.

Right: The third prototype Avro 555 Bison, N155, is at Martlesham Heath in January 1923. Note the portholes in front of the large observation window, the former being unique to the first three prototypes and the Mk Is and Mk IAs. After extensive trials, N155 joined 423 Flight in November 1923 and remained in service until March 1929. (Martyn Chorlton)

Below: The pilot of the Bison had an outstanding forward field of vision as shown with Mk II N9948 '21' of 423 Flight. The aircraft would have been jointly operated from either HMS *Argus* or *Hermes* between May 1925 and September 1926. (Martyn Chorlton)

549 Aldershot Mk I to IV

Development

Produced to Air Ministry specification 2/20 (DoR Type 4B), the Avro 549 Aldershot was the company's first entirely new military aircraft since the end of World War One. Designed by Roy Chadwick, the Aldershot was trialled head-to-head with the de Havilland Derby, a competition it would ultimately win for the small prize of re-equipping a single RAF squadron for just 16 months.

Design

The Aldershot was the first Avro aircraft to have an all-metal fuselage, which was large enough to incorporate a plywood-covered central cabin with two floors. Power was provided by a single 650hp Rolls-Royce Condor in the prototypes and the Mk III production aircraft. The aircraft was crewed by two pilots in an open cockpit with dual controls aft of the mainplanes; behind was the rear gunner with a Scarff ring-mounted Lewis machine gun, and below in the cabin was a bomb aimer and radio operator.

The Aldershot was fitted with slightly swept three-bay wings of wooden construction, which folded to the rear. The big ailerons were aerodynamically balanced by using 'park bench' aerofoils on the top of the upper mainplane.

Two prototypes were built as Mk Is, but the first, J6852, was later converted to Mk II standard with a 1,000hp Napier Cub engine at a huge cost of £10,000. The Cub was so powerful Chadwick had to redesign the engine mountings and strengthen the fuselage. The definitive production version, the Mk III, featured a longer fuselage, a stronger undercarriage and fuel tanks mounted under the upper mainplane. The latter modification made room for an internal bomb load of up to 2,000lb. The final version saw J6852 converted again, this time to Mk IV standard with an 850hp Beardmore Typhoon I engine. This aircraft proved to be longest surviving example, and remained in its test bed role until December 1927.

Service

Reformed on 1 April 1924 with the Vickers Vimy, the only recipient of the Aldershot Mk III was 99 Squadron based at Bircham Newton, Norfolk, which began to receive the type in August. The big, single-engined heavy bombers were popular with the crews and were particularly adept at night flying owing to the aircraft's excellent stability. The squadron took part in the RAF Display flypast at Hendon on 27 June 1925, but not long after the Air Ministry began to reconsider the idea of having such a large aircraft in service with a single engine. The squadron's excellent safety record with the type, which saw not one engine or mechanical failure occur, did nothing to stop the decision to replace the Aldershot with the twin-engined Handley Page Hyderabad. In December 1925, the type was withdrawn from 99 Squadron, and aircraft were placed in storage until mid-1926 when the majority were scrapped.

Production

Seventeen Aldershots were built over four marks; two prototypes, J6852 and J6852, were originally built as Mk Is, but the former was rebuilt twice as the Mk II and Mk IV. Production aircraft were built in two batches of three (J6942–J6944) and 15 aircraft (J6945–J6956), respectively.

Technical data – 549 Aldershot Mk I to IV	
ENGINE	(Mk I & III) One 650hp Rolls-Royce Condor III; (Mk II) One 1,000hp Napier Cub; (Mk IV) One 850hp Beardmore Typhoon I
WINGSPAN	68ft
LENGTH	45ft
HEIGHT	15ft 3in
WING AREA	1,064 sq ft
TARE WEIGHT	(Mk III) 6,310lb
ALL-UP WEIGHT	(Mk III) 10,950lb
MAX SPEED	(Mk III) 110mph
CRUISING SPEED	(Mk III) 92mph
SERVICE CEILING	14,500ft
RANGE	625 miles

Above: The longest serving Aldershot of all was the first prototype, J6852, seen here in its final Mk IV form as a test bed for the 850hp Beardmore Typhoon I engine. The aircraft was redesignated fully as the 549C Mk IV and first flew with the Typhoon on 10 January 1927. (Martyn Chorlton)

Right: Out of the 17 Aldershots built, 14 of them (J6943 to J6956) served with 99 Squadron at Bircham Newton between August 1924 and December 1925, including J6947. (Martyn Chorlton)

557 Ava

Development

The 557 Ava was designed to a specification that called for a long-range coastal patrol aircraft that could also be used as a night bomber. Originally designated by Avro as the 556 torpedo bomber, this role was later dispensed with, but the ability to carry a large Whitehead torpedo below the fuselage had already influenced the size of the design. However, during the development of the aircraft, the goal posts were moved when the Admiralty introduced the smaller 18in Mk VIII torpedo, and the dimensions of the aircraft were deemed unnecessary.

Design

Designed to specification 16/22 (DoR Type 9) by Roy Chadwick, the idea for this large torpedo bomber came about in November 1921. The bombing role mentioned earlier was removed while the aircraft was being constructed, so the first prototype, serialled N171, was finished off as a coastal machine. Built entirely from wood, the 557 Ava had folding wings and the two pilots, seated side-by-side, had dual controls. The aircraft was equipped with three air gunner positions: one in the extreme nose, which dropped away at an angle of 45 degrees, resulting in a beak-shaped forward fuselage; a second was placed in the dorsal position behind the mainplane; and, directly below, a third retractable position was installed. All could be mounted with a single .303in Lewis machine gun, but no weapons were ever installed. The 557 Ava could also carry up to 2,000lb of bombs and a single 21in Whitehead torpedo positioned between the main undercarriage directly below the fuselage.

The 557 Ava was powered by a pair of 650hp Rolls-Royce Condor III water-cooled engines, which were gravity fed by fuel from tanks located directly above them. Also worthy of mention was the aircraft's rudders, which were the largest examples to date of the unique Avro comma-type. Initially, these were incorporated into a triple fin arrangement, but this was soon reduced to two.

Service

Both Avas undertook their maiden flights from Hamble; N171 taking to the air first in mid-1924 but was not trialled at Martlesham Heath until April 1925. This aircraft remained out of the public eye until 3 July 1926, when it appeared in the New Types Park at Hendon numbered '14'. By January 1927, N171 was back at Martlesham, but after magneto failure work with the Ava came to an abrupt end. A second prototype, serialled N172, first flew on 22 April 1927, and this aircraft also made its first public

Technical data – 557 Ava	
ENGINE	Two 650hp Rolls-Royce Condor III
WINGSPAN	(N171) 96ft 10; (N172) 95ft 4in
LENGTH	61ft 9in
HEIGHT	19ft 7¾in
WING AREA	2,163 sq ft
TARE WEIGHT	(N171) 12,760lb; (N172) 13,304lb
ALL-UP WEIGHT	(N171) 19,920lb; (N172) 20,465lb
MAX SPEED	115mph

appearance at Hendon on 2 July 1927. Later in July the aircraft was being trialled by 22 Squadron and the A&AEE, but on 2 August, the aircraft forced landed at Ramsey St Mary, Huntingdonshire, and never flew again.

Production
Only two prototypes were built: one to specification 16/22 (originally DoR Type 9) serialled N171, and N172 to contract No.356442/22 on 18 October 1923.

Right: The first of two Avro 557 Ava 'Torpedo Bomber Tractor Biplanes', N171 is seen here at Martlesham Heath at the beginning of A&AEE performance trials in April 1925. (Martyn Chorlton)

Below: The second prototype, N172, in the New Types Park at Hendon on 2 July 1927, displaying the number '5'. Four weeks later, the big aircraft force landed in Huntingdonshire and never flew again. (Martyn Chorlton)

561 Andover

Development

By the early to mid-1920s, the RAF's DH.10s were already becoming rather tired, having been plying the Cairo–Baghdad air route for many years. Its replacement would be the versatile 561 Andover, which could be operated as a traditional 12-passenger airliner or alternatively as an air ambulance. By the time the Andover was ready, the desert air route was transferred to Imperial Airways, and the RAF only ordered three machines.

Design

The Andover drew heavily from the Aldershot; the latter's folding wings, tail and undercarriage were used, while the fuselage was a completely new design. Constructed in three sections, the cabin section of the fuselage was 22ft long, 4ft 9in wide and 6ft high and was shaped using oval rings and stringers covered on both sides by plywood. The gap created between the two plywood surfaces helped to control temperature variations and also provide part insulation against noise. There was room for 12 passengers seated in wicker chairs, six either side of a central gangway or alternatively six stretcher cases.

Overall, the fuselage was made up of a forward steel-tube cantilever engine mount with a section containing a large radiator behind, complete with shutters. A wooden monocoque cabin completed the central section, and a tubular-steel rear section, covered in fabric, tapered away towards the tail. The pilot flew the Andover from an open cockpit positioned below the leading edge of the upper mainplane, while the navigator sat on his right and slightly below. An access panel near the navigator's position led to the front of the passenger cabin via a door through the front bulkhead.

Power was provided by a single 650hp Rolls-Royce Condor III engine, which was fed fuel by gravity from a pair of slipper-tanks mounted on top the wing.

Service

The first of three Andovers ordered for the RAF, serialled J7261, made its maiden flight in 1924. Displaying number '8' on the fuselage, the aircraft made its first public appearance in the New Types Park at Hendon, and at the RAF Display, also at Hendon, J7261 took part in the air display. All three aircraft had entered RAF service at Halton by late 1924.

A single civilian variant of the aircraft, designated the 563 Andover, was ordered by the Air Ministry. The aircraft become the first Avro machine to be specifically ordered for airline service and only differed by having a toilet and space for luggage towards the rear of the machine. Registered as G-EBKW, the aircraft was loaned to Imperial Airways, which used the aircraft for cross-Channel proving flights before it was ultimately transferred to the RAF.

Production

Four 561 Andovers were built, the first three to contract 458918/23 for the RAF and serialled J7261 to J7263. The fourth aircraft was built as civilian 563 Andover and initially registered as G-EBKW for brief service with Imperial Airways. By January 1927, the aircraft had transferred to the RAF and was serialled J7264.

Technical data – 561 Andover	
ENGINE	One 650hp Rolls-Royce Condor III
WINGSPAN	68ft; (folded) 27ft 6in
LENGTH	51ft 3in
HEIGHT	15ft 3in
WING AREA	1,062 sq ft
TARE WEIGHT	6,980lb
ALL-UP WEIGHT	11,500lb
MAX SPEED	110mph
SERVICE CEILING	13,500ft
RANGE	460 miles

Right: The first of three Andovers built for the RAF was J7261, which was operated at Halton from April 1925. (Martyn Chorlton)

Below: The fourth Andover was ordered by the Air Council and built as the Avro 563 for Imperial Airways. Registered as G-EBKW, the aircraft only gave brief civilian service before being transferred to the RAF as J7264. (Martyn Chorlton)

571 & 572 Buffalo Mk I & II

Development

A private venture, the Avro 571 Buffalo was built in response to specification 21/23, which called for a deck-landing, torpedo-carrying bombing landplane. The specification was designed to replace the Blackburn Dart, a tough call considering the competition was the Handley Page H.P.31 Harrow and the favourite, the excellent Blackburn Ripon.

Design

Powered by a 450hp Napier Lion VA, the Buffalo was single-bay folding wing biplane that inherited a great deal of the mainplane structure of the Bison Mk II. Spruce was used for the wing spars, and again in the ribs in combination with duralumin. Only one set of ailerons were installed on the lower mainplane. The tail unit made use of the Bison's fin and rudder, and the tailplane could be adjusted for incidence. The sturdy undercarriage had a wide-track and was fitted with long-travel oleos combined with 'rubber-compression' shock absorbers.

The tubular steel fuselage covered with duralumin decking and fabric sides was a design unique to the Buffalo. Thought was given to the pilot occupying a high position in the aircraft so that his forward vision was good for carrier landings. Behind the pilot, a second crew member had access to a radio cabin and a prone position for when he took on the role of bomb aimer. The same crewman was expected to defend the aircraft as well and a Scarff-mounted pair of twin Lewis machine guns were supplied for this task. As with the Bison, floatation bags were fitted, and the main fuel tank had a dump valve so that it could provide extra buoyancy when empty.

Service

The 571 Buffalo Mk I, registered as G-EBNW, first flew from Hamble in 1926 and was trialled by the A&AEE that October. The trials for specification 21/23 saw the Ripon reign supreme, the Buffalo being rejected because of poor handling. To rectify this, the Buffalo Mk I was flown back to Hamble where a range of modifications were implemented. Firstly, the wings were replaced by all-metal ones which were more rectangular, and four Frise ailerons and Handley Page slots were also fitted. Re-engined with a 530hp Napier Lion XIA, the aircraft re-emerged as the 572 Buffalo Mk II still registered as G-EBNW. The aircraft was back at the A&AEE by December 1927, where it is presumed the aircraft handled much better but by then competition was well and truly over.

In July 1928, G-EBNW was purchased by the Air Ministry, serialled N239 and converted into a seaplane and trialled at the Marine Aircraft Experimental Establishment (MAEE) at Felixstowe. The aircraft was later transferred to the Development Flight at Gosport, but little is known about the aircraft beyond 1930.

Technical data – 571 Buffalo Mk I & 572 Buffalo Mk II	
ENGINE	(571) One 450hp Napier Lion VA; (572) One 530hp Napier Lion XIA
WINGSPAN	46ft
LENGTH	36ft 6in
HEIGHT	15ft 3in
WING AREA	684 sq ft
TARE WEIGHT	4,233lb
ALL-UP WEIGHT	7,430lb
MAX SPEED	135mph
CRUISING SPEED	105mph
INITIAL CLIMB RATE	770ft/min
SERVICE CEILING	13,700ft
RANGE	650 miles

Above: The Buffalo, in its second form as the 572 Mk II, is seen here at the A&AEE, Martlesham Heath, in December 1927. (Martyn Chorlton)

Right: The 572 Mk II Buffalo at Hamble in 1927, with rectangular wingtips and Frise ailerons on each mainplane. The Handley Page slots can just be seen at the front of the upper mainplane. (Martyn Chorlton)

584 Avocet

Development

The 583 Avocet was a purposeful looking, all-metal stressed-skin sesquiplane, which was designed to meet a specification for a new fleet fighter. Unfortunately, due to the lack of power installed, the aircraft failed to impress, and no production order was placed.

Design

Designed to Air Ministry specification 17/25, which was issued in June 1926, the Avocet was a single-seat fighter, which featured some very pleasant design features. The fuselage in particular was very sleek and slim thanks to its stressed-skin, which was wrapped around a constant diameter alloy tube that tapered away towards the tail. Covered in a number of riveted duralumin sheets, the fuselage was mounted mid-way between the 29ft-span upper wing and the shorter lower wing. The wing structure comprised a single-bay separated by N-type interplane struts, while full-span Frise ailerons were mounted on the upper wing only. Power was provided by a supercharged 180hp Armstrong Siddeley Lynx IV that drove a metal propeller.

The Avocet also offered the FAA versatility as the fighter could be fitted with a wheeled undercarriage for operations from a carrier or twin floats, which gave the extra option of being catapulted from a cruiser. Several catapult points were engineered into the fuselage and strain on the pilot's neck during the launch was relieved by a substantial head-rest behind the cockpit. When the aircraft was retrieved from the water during cruiser operations, a sturdy pick-up ring was built into the upper wing just forward of the cockpit; the strain being transferred through two substantial struts that were fitted into the upper forward fuselage.

Armament was a pair of Vickers machine guns mounted on each side of the forward fuselage, both synchronised to fire through the propeller.

Service

Only two prototypes were ever built, the first, serialled N209, made its maiden flight from Hamble on wheels in December 1927, followed by the second aircraft, N210, which first flew on floats in May 1928. The two aircraft only differed by having dissimilar shaped tail surfaces; N209 had a triangular-shaped fin and unbalanced rudder, while N210 had a small fin and very large horn-balanced rudder. In June 1928, N210 was also fitted with a wheeled undercarriage, and in February 1929, both aircraft were delivered to the A&AEE, Martlesham Heath, for evaluation by the FAA. It seems that the test pilots of the A&AEE were unimpressed with the performance of the Avocet, which could have handled a much more powerful engine. However, a military role for N210 was found when, in September 1929, the aircraft had its floats refitted and the Avocet joined the RAF's High Speed Flight at Calshot. There, the aircraft made an ideal practice aircraft for the Flight's Schneider Trophy Pilots.

Technical data – 584 Avocet	
ENGINE	One 180hp Armstrong Siddeley Lynx IV
WINGSPAN	29ft
LENGTH	(N209 float) 27ft 6in; (N210 wheels) 24ft 6in
HEIGHT	(N209 float) 11ft 10in; (N210 wheels) 11ft 8⅜in
WING AREA	308 sq ft
TARE WEIGHT	(N209 landplane) 1,621lb; (N210 landplane) 1,669lb
ALL-UP WEIGHT	2,495lb
MAX SPEED	(wheels) 133mph
SERVICE CEILING	23,000ft
ARMAMENT	Two .303in Vickers machine-guns

This was the second of only two Avro 584 Avocet 'Fleet Fighter Tractor Biplanes' ordered to Air Ministry specification 17/25. Originally built as a seaplane, N210 is undertaking landplane trials at the A&AEE in July 1928. The aircraft later reverted to floats and served with the High Speed Flight at Calshot. (Martyn Chorlton)

604 Antelope

Development

By the late 1920s, the criteria of the Air Ministry specifications appeared to be running away from the technology available, and one such example, issued in May 1926, demanded that a day bomber should have a top speed of 160mph! Such a speed was initially deemed impossible, but Avro rose to the challenge, in the face of some very stiff competition, in the shape of the excellent Fairey Fox and the Hawker Hart; all three aircraft would become the most advanced military biplanes of the period.

Design

Avro responded to specification 12/26 for a two-seat, high-performance day bomber by designing the 604 Antelope to contract 762628/27. Power was, at first, provided by the eight-cylinder 480hp Rolls-Royce F.XIB V-type water-cooled engine; one of the most powerful aero engines readily available. The F.XIB drove a Fairey F.R.608 fixed-pitch propeller and cooling was provided by a radiator mounted directly under the engine with the air intake controlled by shutters. Fuel was provided by a 65-gallon main tank backed up by a 25-gallon gravity tank, both mounted directly behind the engine.

A single-bay biplane, the Antelope had a set of Frise ailerons fitted to the upper mainplane only; the lower mainplane was 4ft shorter and had a much narrower chord. The wings, which were slightly staggered and swept, were made from metal and covered in fabric. The upper mainplane wing roots tapered at their attachment point to give the pilot improved forward vision. Behind the pilot was the air gunner's cockpit, complete with a .303in Lewis machine gun, which was mounted on a patented Avro-designed gun ring that was wind-balanced. The Antelope also had a fixed, forward-firing Vickers machine gun and bombs were carried on racks mounted under the lower mainplane. These were aimed by the air gunner, who was provided with a prone position in the lower fuselage of the aircraft.

Service

First flown in August 1928, the sole Antelope, serialled J9183, was sent to Martlesham Heath for evaluation on 13 September. Despite the Antelope and the Fox Mk II being excellent aircraft, only the Hart was ordered into production.

After making a public appearance at the Olympia Airshow, between 16 and 27 July 1929, the Antelope joined 100 Squadron at Bicester for service trials, even though a main production contract was not secured. Back at Hamble, in July 1930, the aircraft was fitted with dual controls, and, not long after, the Antelope joined the RAE at Farnborough as a Gloster-Hele-Shaw-Beacham variable pitch propeller test bed. During this trial, the Antelope was re-engined twice, first with a Rolls-Royce Kestrel IB and again with a supercharged Kestrel IIS. Test flying began with the RAE from 29 September 1930, and the Antelope remained in this role at Farnborough until September 1933.

Technical data – 604 Antelope	
ENGINE	One 480hp Rolls-Royce F.XIB, 525hp Kestrel IB or 477hp Kestrel IIS
WINGSPAN	(upper) 36ft; (lower) 32ft
LENGTH	31ft 2in
HEIGHT	10ft 9in
WING AREA	377 sq ft
TARE WEIGHT	(bomber) 2,859lb; (trainer) 2,898lb
ALL-UP WEIGHT	(bomber) 4,538lb; (trainer) 4,550lb
MAX SPEED	(F.XIB) 173mph
CRUISING SPEED	(F.XIB) 145mph
INITIAL CLIMB RATE	(F.XIB) 1,470ft/min
SERVICE CEILING	(F.XIB) 22,000ft
RANGE	(F.XIB) 580 miles

The sole Antelope at the A&AEE during the aircraft's performance trials, which were conducted between September 1928 and January 1929. (Martyn Chorlton)

621 Tutor & 646 Sea Tutor

Development

The Avro 621 Tutor was the result of three years' worth of competitive trials for the prize of replacing the RAF's 504N as its main elementary trainer from 1932. The Tutor's success would continue to run with a tradition that began during World War One, when the 504K and J were also accepted by the fledgling RAF in the same role.

Design

Designed in 1929 by Roy Chadwick, the original Avro 621 was a two-seat basic trainer powered by a five-cylinder Armstrong Siddeley Mongoose engine. The aircraft was constructed of welded steel, which was found to be more advantageous, especially in extreme climates, than wooden-built machines. The conventional looking 621 had staggered all-metal, fabric-covered, equal-span wings and a horn-balanced rudder similar to the Avro Avian.

The production 621 Tutor for the RAF differed externally by having a Townend ring fitted around a Lynx IV or IVC engine. The undercarriage was slightly repositioned with Dunlop low-pressure tyres (later replaced by Goodyear Airwheels) and Frise-type ailerons were fitted to all four wings.

The 646 Sea Tutor, built to specification 26/34 and 17/33 (the latter for the floats), was fitted with a pair of floats. Only 15 were built, all serving with the MAEE at Felixstowe and the Seaplane Training Flight at Calshot.

Service

A batch of 21 Mongoose-powered 621s entered the RAF for service trials at Gosport and 3 FTS at Grantham in 1930. Prior to the RAF committing to full production of the 621 Tutor, these original aircraft served well and were not fully retired until 1937.

Deliveries of the 626 Tutor to the RAF began in October 1931 when the first 16 production aircraft were issued to 3 FTS. The aircraft was also delivered to the CFS at Upavon, the RAF College at Cranwell and later to 5 FTS at Sealand and 11 FTS at Wittering as the RAF's main primary trainer. By the mid-1930s, the aircraft became the primary equipment of many University Air Squadrons (UAS) and the core of several Auxiliary Air Force squadrons. The type was withdrawn from FTSs from 1939, but a large number remained on RAF strength into World War Two, and quite a few were not struck off charge (SOC) until 1944, while one aircraft, K6118, allocated to 1036 Air Training Corps (ATC) Squadron, clung on until September 1946.

The 626 Tutor also achieved a healthy number of foreign sales including 29 to the Greek Air Force, half a dozen to the RCAF, five to the Kwangsi Air Force, three to the Irish Air Force and two to the Polish Air Force and the South African Air Force (SAAF). In South Africa, a further 57 were built under licence, and three were also built under licence in Denmark.

Production

A trial batch of Avro 621 Trainers, K1230 to K1240 and K1787 to K1797, were built to specification 3/30 before the main production batch of 394 Tutors were built to specification 18/31. Including the Sea Tutor, the main batch of aircraft were serialled K2496 to K2513, K3189 to K3476, K4798 to K4837, K6087 to K6126, K6923 to K6925 and K8168 to K8172.

Technical data – 621 Tutor & 646 Sea Tutor	
ENGINE	One 155hp Armstrong Siddeley Mongoose IIIC (aka IIIA), one 215hp Armstrong Siddeley Lynx IV or Lynx IVC
WINGSPAN	34ft
LENGTH	(621 IIIC) 26ft 7¾in; (621 IVC) 26ft 4½in; (646) 29ft 3in
HEIGHT	(621) 9ft 7in; (646) 11ft 6in
WING AREA	(621 IIIC) 302 sq ft; (621 IVC) 301 sq ft; (646) 300 sq ft
TARE WEIGHT	(621 IIIC) 1,535lb; (621 IVC) 1,844lb; (646) 2,218lb
ALL-UP WEIGHT	(621 IIIC) 2,182lb; (621 IVC) 2,493lb; (646) 2,894lb
MAX SPEED	(621 IIIC) 104mph; (621 IVC) 120mph; (646) 92mph
CRUISING SPEED	(621 IIIC & 646) 95mph; (621 IVC) 97mph
INITIAL CLIMB RATE	(621 IIIC) 725ft/min; (621 IVC) 910ft/min; (646) 430ft/min
SERVICE CEILING	(621 IIIC) 12,400ft; (621 IVC) 16,000ft; (646) 12,000ft
RANGE	(621 IIIC) 380 miles; (621 IVC) 250 miles; (646) 240 miles

One of 40 Tutor Mk Is delivered to the RAF between August and September 1935, K6115 is undertaking an air test in late 1935. The aircraft went on to serve with 'C' Flight, Gosport, 12 Maintenance Unit (MU), 18 MU, the Air Transport Auxiliary (ATA) and No. 4 (Observer) Advanced Flying Unit (4 OAFU) at West Freugh before being struck off charge (SOC) on 25 June 1943. (Martyn Chorlton)

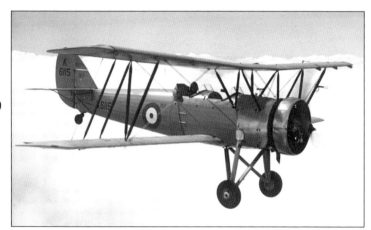

The second of only 14 Sea Tutors built, K3373 only served with 'A' Flight at Calshot from June 1934 to January 1935, when it was written off in an accident after only 68 hours of flying time. (Martyn Chorlton)

626, Prefect & 637

Development

The Avro 626 and subsequent 637 were a successful attempt to provide small air forces across the world with an economical military aircraft. Effectively a slightly redesigned Tutor, the Avro 626 was supplied to the customer with a basic conversion kit that could enable the aircraft to carry out a host of military roles from bombing to blind flying instruction.

Design

The general structure and configuration of the Avro 626 was virtually identical to the Tutor, and it was powered by the same 240hp Lynx IVC engine, although those supplied to Egypt and Brazil were powered by a 260hp Cheetah. The 626 had the luxury of a third cockpit, which could be accessed from the second. This third cockpit could be furnished with wireless equipment and/or air navigation equipment, or have an Avro mounting complete with machine gun for air gunnery training.

Another version, specifically for the RAF, was the Prefect, of which only seven were built to replace the aging Mongoose-powered trainers operating with the School of Air Navigation at Andover. The Prefect was fitted with just two cockpits, had their aileron circuits modified and a tail wheel, rather than a skid attached.

The Avro 637 was designed as a lightly armed frontier patrol aircraft equipped with a single fixed .303in Vickers machine gun for the pilot and a rear gunner with an Avro low-drag mounted .303in Lewis machine gun. Capable of carrying up to 400 rounds of ammunition, six 20lb bombs and a vertical camera, or four 20lb bombs and radio equipment, the Avro 637 was a very versatile aircraft. The 637 had a span 2ft longer than its predecessor, and the wing tips were rounded. Powered by a Cheetah V, the 637 also had an extra fuel tank in the forward fuselage.

Service

As a result of understanding the requirements of foreign air forces, Avro had little trouble in selling the 626 aboard beginning with South America, where 15 served in Argentina, 16 in Brazil and 20 in Chile. The type also served in Austria, Belgium, Czechoslovakia, Egypt, Estonia, Greece, Ireland, Portugal, Slovakia and Spain. A dozen served with the RCAF's 3 and 111 squadrons, all being converted with enclosed heated cockpits, skis and an Arctic engine cowling.

The Prefect joined the RAF in June 1935 (K5063 to K5069), the majority of them serving with 48 Squadron from March 1936. Taken out of service in 1939, just like the Tutor, some examples were not SOC until 1946. Four Prefects also served with the RNZAF from July 1935, but as they had a third cockpit, these were often referred to as Avro 626s.

Only eight Avro 637s were built, all of them being supplied to the Kwangsi Air Force, Luchow, South China by the Far East Aviation Co. Ltd in Hong Kong.

Technical data – 626 Prefect landplane & 637	
ENGINE	(626) One 215hp Armstrong Siddeley Lynx IVC or one 260hp Armstrong Siddeley Cheetah V; (637) One 260hp Armstrong Siddeley Cheetah V
WINGSPAN	(626) 34ft; (637) 36ft
LENGTH	(626) 26ft 6in; (637) 27ft 3in
HEIGHT	(626) 9ft 7in; (637) 9ft 9in
WING AREA	(626) 300 sq ft; (637) 314 sq ft
TARE WEIGHT	(626 Lynx) 1,765lb; (626 Cheetah) 2,010lb; (637) 1,987lb
ALL-UP WEIGHT	(626 Lynx) 2,750lb; (626 Cheetah) 2,667lb; (637) 3,127lb
MAX SPEED	(626 Lynx) 112mph; (626 Cheetah) 130mph; (637) 135mph
CRUISING SPEED	(626 Lynx) 95mph; (626 Cheetah) 108mph; (637) 115mph
INITIAL CLIMB RATE	(626 Lynx) 880ft/min; (626 Cheetah) 1,000ft/min; (637) 990ft/min
SERVICE CEILING	(626 Lynx) 14,800ft; (626 Cheetah) 16,800ft; (637) 16,000ft
RANGE	(626 Lynx) 240 miles; (626 Cheetah) 210 miles; (637) 540 miles

First demonstrated in Brazil in 1933, the country was so impressed it ordered 16 Avro 626s for its air force. (Martyn Chorlton)

One of the many features of the Avro 637 was a tunnel-type windscreen that helped to protect the pilot from the elements while the rear gunner's position, complete with Avro low-drag mounting for the machine gun, was completely exposed. After being initially assigned civilian 'VH-' registrations, all 637s were given military serials on joining the Kwangsi Air Force. (Martyn Chorlton)

671 Rota Mk I (Cierva C.30A)

Development

In 1934, Avro struck a deal with the Cierva Autogiro Company to build, under licence, the two-seat C.30A at Manchester. Intending to build the aircraft for the civilian market, the first production order actually came from the Air Ministry.

Design

The C.30A was a radial-engined autogiro powered by the Genet Major I engine with a 37ft-long three-bladed rotor, positioned on a pyramidal rotor, mounted on four legs. The aircraft had two cockpits with dual-controls, a fabric-covered fuselage and an unbraced tailplane. The Avro version differed from the original Cierva by having a wider track undercarriage, different strutting, a braced tailplane and small trim able surfaces on the tailplane and fin.

By the time specification 16/35 had been issued by the Air Ministry, deliveries were already being made and the order increased from ten to 12 aircraft. One additional order was for K4296, which was used for Short S.61 float trials, the machine making is maiden flight from the River Medway on 15 April 1935.

Service

The first Rota Mk I, K4230, flew in 1934 and was initially issued to the Directorate of Technical Development before proceeding to Martlesham Heath for service trials in February 1935. The rest of the production order was delivered to the School of Army Co-Operation (SAC) at Old Sarum between August 1934 and May 1935. Individual aircraft were passed to army co-operation squadrons for trials with the army, but by the beginning of World War Two only four remained serviceable. To supplement these, five civilian C.30As were impressed into military service and serialled AP506 to AP510. These aircraft, including the Rota Mk Is, were dispersed between the Special Duties Flight, Calibration Flight, and the Autogiro Section of 74 (Signals) Wing; the latter, under the command of Sqn Ldr R. A. C. Brie, was stationed at Duxford.

All of these units were amalgamated into 1448 Flight. Formed at Duxford on 17 February 1942, the flight was tasked with radar calibration, which it conducted for every radar station from the Isle of Wight to the Orkneys. The flight moved to Halton on 2 Marchand was redesignated as 529 (Rota) Squadron on 15 June 1943.

529 Squadron, the RAF's only specialist autogiro unit, remained at Halton until 18 August 1944 when it moved to Henley (Crazies Hill). The unit was active with the Rota Mk I until October 1945, when it disbanded, and the autogiros were placed on the civilian market.

Production

Ten Avro Rota Mk I were initially ordered to contract 294074/33; serialled K4230 to K4239, these aircraft were delivered between August 1934 and May 1935. Two further aircraft were ordered, firstly K4296, which was built as the sole Rota Seaplane, and K4775, as a standard machine, delivered in January 1935. Further orders, serialled K6553 and K6554, were cancelled and a planned Rota Mk II, K7286, was also shelved. The five ex-civilian aircraft, AP506 to AP510, were impressed in June 1940 to contract B50801/40.

Technical data – 671 Rota Mk I	
ENGINE	One 140hp Armstrong Siddeley Genet Major IA
ROTOR DIAMETER	37ft
LENGTH	19ft 8½in
HEIGHT	11ft 1in
TARE WEIGHT	1,220lb
ALL-UP WEIGHT	1,900lb
MAX SPEED	110mph
CRUISING SPEED	95mph
INITIAL CLIMB RATE	700ft/min
SERVICE CEILING	6,600ft
RANGE	285 miles

The first of only 12 Avro Rota Mk Is was K4230, displaying New Types number '15' from its appearance in public at Hendon in 1934. The machine was put through rigorous trials with the A&AEE followed by deck landing trials aboard HMS *Courageous* and *Furious* during July and September 1935. The autogiro was also briefly operated by 2 Squadron before it was SOC in March 1939. (Martyn Chorlton)

Several Rotas were allocated to fixed-wing RAF army co-operation squadrons for trials, including K4239, which served with 26 Squadron from February 1936 to February 1939. This autogiro enjoyed a busy military career that ended on 1 August 1946, when the aircraft was sold to F. C. Bettison of Grantham. (Martyn Chorlton)

652A Anson Mk I

Development

The remarkable story of the Avro 652 Anson first came about in May 1933 from an Imperial Airways requirement for a twin-engined aircraft capable of carrying four passengers at a cruising speed of 150mph over a distance of 600 miles. During the design stage of 652, the Air Ministry coincidentally made a request for a twin-engine coastal patrol aircraft, whose specification was almost identical to that of Imperial Airways. On 19 May 1934, the design, designated the 652A, was submitted to the Air Ministry.

Design

A low-wing monoplane with retractable undercarriage and powered by a pair of cowled Cheetah engines, the Avro 652A was a good-looking aircraft. Provision was made for a single hand-operated turret directly above the main spar, which was fitted with a .303in Lewis machine gun. The pilot was also equipped with a single forward-firing .303in Vickers machine gun and the 652A was capable of carrying up to 360lb in bombs in the centre section of the aircraft. Other changes from the civilian 652 were square rather than oval windows and an access door on the starboard side of the fuselage.

When the Air Ministry adopted the 652A, it was officially known as the Anson Mk I and apart from a slightly longer span tailplane, smaller elevators, larger cabin windows and, later, more powerful 350hp Cheetah IX engines, the aircraft was altered little from the original remit. As production continued, further modifications, such as metal-framed ailerons, steeper windscreens with direct-vision panels and Schrenk hydraulic flaps were also introduced.

Service

The prototype 652A, K4772, was first flown by Bill Thorn on 24 March 1935, followed by the first production machine, K6152, by Geoffrey Tyson from Woodford on 31 December 1935. The first Ansons for the RAF were delivered to 48 Squadron at Manston in February 1936, the type making history by becoming the first monoplane with a retractable undercarriage to join the service. These early Mk Is were capable of carrying a pair of 100lb and four 20lb bombs plus smoke floats and flares. The type saw a great deal of action during the early stages of the war, including attacking a U-boat and shooting down a Do 18 flying boat – and even a pair of Bf 109s over the English Channel in June 1940!

Forty-eight operational RAF squadrons would go on to receive the Anson Mk I, and hundreds of second line units would continue to fly the Mk I well into the post-war period.

Overseas, the RAAF were the first recipients of the Anson Mk I in late 1936, followed by the Finnish and Estonian Air Forces, the Irish Air Corps and the Turkish, Greek and Iraqi Air Forces before war broke out.

A trainer version of the Anson Mk I, with a dorsal turret, complete with flaps entered service from the spring of 1939 and became the standard multi-engine trainer in Canada and Australia as part of the Commonwealth Air Training Plan.

Production

There were 7,195 Anson Mk Is built in 12 production batches between 1935 and 1945.

Technical data – 652A Anson Mk I	
ENGINE	Two 335hp Armstrong Siddeley Cheetah IX
WINGSPAN	56ft 6in
LENGTH	42ft 3in
HEIGHT	13ft 1in
WING AREA	463 sq ft
TARE WEIGHT	5,375lb
ALL-UP WEIGHT	7,665lb
MAX SPEED	188mph
CRUISING SPEED	158mph
INITIAL CLIMB RATE	960ft/min
SERVICE CEILING	19,000ft
RANGE	660 miles

Ordered in 1938, Anson Mk I N5331 was one of 500 built from the sixth production batch for the RAF, which was delivered between October 1938 and September 1939. Available in huge numbers even before the war broke out, very few of this batch made it to operational units. However, one that did was N5331, which served with 27 Elementary and Reserve Flying Training School (ERFTS), 10 Flying Training School (FTS), 6 Air Observers Navigation School (AONS), 6 Air Observers School (AOS) and 10 Radio School (RS) until March 1945. (*Aeroplane*)

Re-formed on 15 March 1937 at Boscombe Down, 217 Squadron operated the Anson Mk I in the general reconnaissance role with Coastal Command until December 1940. (*Aeroplane*)

643 Mk II Cadet

Development
A slightly smaller version of the Tutor, the 631 and later 643 Mk II Cadet, were designed to be more economical to operate than their established military cousin. The 631 certainly made quite an impression on the Irish Air Corps when it first appeared in late 1931, and they ordered six aircraft straight from the drawing board. The Irish Air Corps ordered a seventh machine, but this was as far as the military sales went for the 631; however, the 643 Mk II Cadet would prove to be more successful.

Design
The 643 Mk II Cadet was the definitive variant of the small Cadet family, which was powered by a 150hp Genet Major IA engine. To enable this more powerful engine to be fitted into the 643 Cadet airframe, the forward fuselage was lengthened by 6in, and to help soak up the extra horsepower the wing spars were made stronger. Further strengthening was achieved by repositioning the bracing wires to the leading wing root, which also served to make an exit from the forward cockpit by parachute a much safer affair. All Mk II Cadets built for the RAAF were also fitted with tail wheels, inverted fuel systems and blind flying equipment.

Service
The prototype 643 Mk II, G-ADJT, first appeared in September 1935, and following a few private sales a good order for 20 aircraft was received from Air Training Services. All of the latter saw service with 3 Elementary and Reserve Flying Training School (ERFTS, later 3 EFTS) at Hamble and 9 ERFTS (later 9 EFTS) at Ansty, wearing civilian registrations.

The RAAF took delivery of 34 Mk II Cadets, all of them initially serving with 1 FTS at Point Cook, 21 (City of Melbourne) and 22 (City of Sydney) Citizen Air Force Squadrons and later the CFS based at Camden. A large number of the Australian-based aircraft survived their service with the RAAF and were sold onto the civilian market in 1946.

Production
First military order for the 631 Cadet was six for the Irish Air Corps (C.1 to C.6) plus a seventh (C.7) ordered at a later date. Thirty-four Avro 643 Mk II Cadets were built at Manchester for the Australian Air Board and delivered in three batches in November 1935, December 1936 and February 1939. These aircraft were allocated the RAAF serials A6-1 to A6-34.

Technical data – 643 Mk II Cadet	
ENGINE	One 150hp Armstrong Siddeley Genet Major IA or one 220hp Jacobs R-755
WINGSPAN	30ft 2in
LENGTH	24ft 9in
HEIGHT	8ft 10in
WING AREA	262 sq ft
TARE WEIGHT	1,286lb
ALL-UP WEIGHT	2,000lb
MAX SPEED	116mph
CRUISING SPEED	100mph
INITIAL CLIMB RATE	700ft/min
SERVICE CEILING	12,000ft
RANGE	325 miles

Avro 643 Mk II Cadets of the RAAF's Central Flying School (CFS) put on a fine display over RAAF Camden on 12 September 1940. (Martyn Chorlton)

636, 636A & 667

Development

An attractive, purposeful looking machine, the Roy Chadwick-designed Avro 636 should have been more successful than it was. Only the Irish Air Corps, as with all aircraft with an Avro 621 lineage, purchased four examples in December 1934 – once again straight from the drawing board.

Design

Designed in late 1934, the 636 was a staggered single-bay biplane that used tensile steel strip for the construction of the spars and ribs. The wings and tailplane utilised the Armstrong Whitworth system of riveting, which was an indication that Avro was now part of the Hawker Siddeley Group.

Each wing was fitted with Frise ailerons, and power was to be provided by a 430hp Armstrong Siddeley Jaguar IV. The structure of the fuselage was made from welded steel-tube and virtually all controls, cables and oil lines could be accessed via fabric-covered curved panels (a throwback to the Tutor). All of the aircraft's fuel was carried in the forward fuselage, leaving the upper wing uncluttered and, like the rest of the 636 family, remarkable clean. The undercarriage was fitted with low-pressure types and Dunlop brake drums, which were barely noticeable thanks to some cleverly designed fairings.

The 636 was a two-seater, designed for fighter pilot training and as such the rear cockpit could be faired over. In the fighter role, the aircraft was fitted with a pair of .303in Vickers machine guns, mounted in the front of a raised deck, which also served to heighten the position of the cockpits well above the engine cowling. In this dedicated fighter role, the aircraft was to be designated the 636A, with extra power provided by a 680hp Panther XI.

Service

The first 636 built was to be a civilian demonstrator registered as G-ADHP; however, work on this machine was abandoned in May 1935, leaving an order for just four aircraft placed by the Irish Air Corps

Technical data – 636, 636A & 667	
ENGINE	(636) One 420hp Armstrong Siddeley Jaguar IV; (636A) One 680hp Armstrong Siddeley Panther XI; (667) One 460hp Armstrong Siddeley Jaguar VIC
WINGSPAN	(upper) 33ft; (lower) 27ft 3in
LENGTH	27ft 6in
HEIGHT	11ft 7in
WING AREA	261 sq ft
TARE WEIGHT	(636A) 2,970lb; (667) 2,766lb
ALL-UP WEIGHT	(636A) 3,924lb; (667) 3,721lb
MAX SPEED	(636A) 230mph; (667) 175mph
CRUISING SPEED	(636A) 195mph
INITIAL CLIMB RATE	(636A) 2,000ft/min; (667) 1,200ft/min
SERVICE CEILING	(636A) 32,000ft; (667) 18,000ft
RANGE	(636A) 290 miles

in November 1934. Although Avro designated the Irish Air Corps aircraft as the 667, they were always still known as 636s and were powered by the 460hp Jaguar VIC engine. These engines were actually old units originally procured for four Vickers Vespa IVs supplied to the Free State in March 1934.

The four aircraft, serialled A.14 to A.17, were delivered to Baldonnel between 15 and 20 October 1935. The 636 was well-liked by all who flew it, the controls being light and responsive and despite having less horsepower than was originally planned the little biplane had a top speed of 175mph.

Initially serving with the IAC Training School at Baldonnel, A.16 was written off in March 1938 followed by A.15 in February 1940. The two remaining aircraft were transferred to 1 (Fighter) Squadron, also at Baldonnel, from where the last example, A.17 (by then serialled just '17') was withdrawn from use in October 1941.

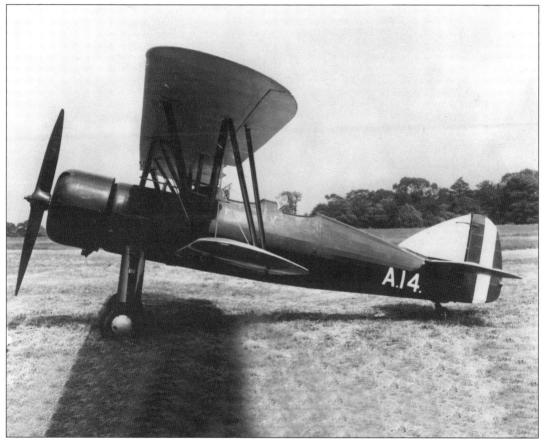

This was the first of just four Avro 636s delivered to the Irish Air Corps in October 1935, which served at Baldonnel until 1941. (Martyn Chorlton)

679 Manchester Mk I & Mk IA

Development

Designed in 1937 to specification P.13/36, in which the Air Ministry called for a new generation of twin-engined bombers, the Avro 679 was the second company aircraft to receive the name Manchester. The specification was hotly contested, but only the Avro 679 and the Handley Page H.P.56 reached the prototype stage.

Design

Very advanced for its day, the Manchester was designed for a crew of seven with the capability to carry a large bomb load, at speed, over a great distance. Sporting a mid-wing, the all-metal Manchester was a cantilever monoplane with an advanced twin-spar, flush-riveted wing and a semi-monocoque fuselage. The crew, with the exception of the dorsal and rear gunners, were all clustered together in one forward cabin under a large transparent canopy, fitted with bulletproof glass. Defensive armament was good and consisted of three Nash & Thompson turrets mounting a total of eight .303in Browning machine guns.

Both the Avro 679 and H.P.56 opted for the untested Rolls-Royce Vulture 24-cylinder engine, the largest and most powerful unit produced by the Derby-based manufacturer. The Vulture consisted of two Peregrine engines mounted on a common crankcase with the potential to produce twice the power of the Merlin.

Service

The prototype Manchester, L7246, made its maiden flight from Ringway on 25 July 1939 in the hands of Avro chief test pilot, H. A. Brown. A production order was placed in July 1939 to a new slightly modified specification, followed by the first Manchester entering RAF service with 207 Squadron at Waddington in November 1940. Regardless of the poor reputation the Manchester would eventually have bestowed upon it, the bomber was praised by all who flew it due to its excellent handling qualities.

Operations began on 24/25 February 1941 to Brest, when half a dozen 207 Squadron Manchesters dropped 500lb SAP bombs on a Hipper-class cruiser in Brest harbour. Raids against German capital ships would become a regular event, and the Manchester also contributed to the first of three 1,000-bomber raids, which saw a posthumous Victoria Cross bestowed upon Manchester pilot Flt Lt T. Manser of 50 Squadron on 30 May/1 June 1942. After completing his bomb run on Cologne, the bomber was struck by flak at 7,000ft, causing the port engine to catch fire. Manser ordered his crew to bale out, keeping the bomber steady while they all escaped with their lives. As well as 50 Squadron, the Manchester also served with 49, 61, 83, 97, 106 and 207 squadrons.

From the outset, the Achilles' heel of the Manchester was its engines; their insufficient development resulted in the Vulture exposing all of its weaknesses whilst flying with operational aircraft. The type's ability to fly on one engine was questionable, although one pilot skilfully managed to fly all the way back from Berlin, but this was a rare example of outstanding airmanship. However, by the late summer of 1941, Manchester losses, especially those through mechanical failure, were no higher than those of the Halifax or Stirling. Regardless, the promising career of the Manchester was brought to an abrupt end, but it was not all to waste for Avro; an iconic development was waiting in the wings.

Production

There were 200 Manchesters ordered to specification 19/37, with work beginning in July 1939 simultaneously at Woodford and the new Metropolitan-Vickers works at Trafford Park for erection at Woodford; 157 were built at the former and 43 at the latter.

Technical data – 679 Manchester Mk I & Mk IA	
ENGINE	(Mk I & IA) Two 1,760 Rolls-Royce Vulture I; (Mk III) Four 1,145hp Merlin X
WINGSPAN	(Proto) 80ft 2in; (Mk I & IA) 90ft 1in
LENGTH	(Proto) 68ft 4in; (Mk I & IA) 68ft 10in
HEIGHT	19ft 6in
WING AREA	(Proto) 1,057½ sq ft; (Mk I & IA) 1,131 sq ft
TARE WEIGHT	(Proto) 25,959lb
ALL-UP WEIGHT	(Proto) 45,000lb; (Mk I) 50,000lb; (Mk IA) 56,000lb
MAX SPEED	(Mk I) 265mph at 17,000ft
CEILING	(Mk I) 19,200ft
RANGE	(Mk I) 1,630 miles with an 8,100lb bomb load; 1,200 miles with a 10,350lb bomb load

Right: Manchester Mk IA R5833 'OL-N' of 83 Squadron has the Welsh inscription 'Ar hyd y nos' ('All through the night') on its nose. It is seen here at Scampton on 8 April 1942. The crew (from left to right) is Sgt J Bushby, Plt Off Billings, Sgt Dodsworth, Sgt Baines, Sgt Williams and their pilot, W/O Whitehead. (*Aeroplane*)

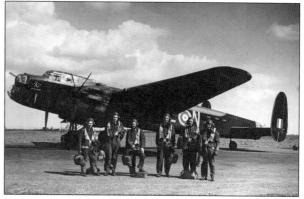

Below: The second Manchester prototype, L7247 was constantly being modified as much as the first aircraft. L7247 is pictured with an interim 'Shark' fin fitted, which was later replaced by a less extreme central fin. Note the lowered dorsal FN.21 turret and the rear FN.4A, which is trained towards the camera. (Martyn Chorlton)

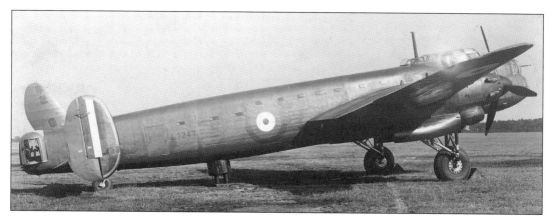

683 Lancaster Mk I & III

Development

There is no hiding the fact that the lineage of the Lancaster was firmly embedded in the Manchester, whose failure, with the benefit of hindsight, resulted in one of the most significant aircraft to serve with the RAF during World War Two. Within a short period of time, the third four-engined 'heavy' to join Bomber Command completely over-shadowed the established Stirling and Halifax, with extraordinary operational statistics and its involvement in high-profile missions.

Design

The hard work of development, including the general layout of the fuselage and aircraft systems, was already in place before it was decided to upgrade the Manchester with four Merlin engines. A single Manchester airframe was withdrawn from the production line and fitted with an enlarged wing, to which four underslung 1,145hp Rolls-Royce Merlin X engines were attached. The prototype, referred to as the Manchester Mk III and serialled BT308, also retained the original bomber's central fin and 22ft tailplane.

First flown from Woodford on 9 January 1941, the aircraft was flown to the A&AEE at Boscombe Down 18 days later. The first production Lancaster Mk I, serialled L7527, made its maiden flight on 31 October 1941. Power was provided by four 1,280hp Merlin XXs driving de Havilland three-bladed, constant-speed propellers that could be fully feathered. The later Mk III only differed through its power-plants, which were American-built Packard Merlin 28 engines, but externally it was identical to the Mk I.

Service

The Lancaster first entered service with 44 (Rhodesia) Squadron at Waddington in December 1941, and its first operation, laying mines in Heligoland Bight, took place on 3 March 1942. More ambitious raids followed beginning on 17 April 1942, when 97 Squadron joined 44 Squadron on a daring low-level daylight raid on the M.A.N. diesel factory at Augsburg, followed by another daylight operation on Le Creusot on October 17.

Within a year of the Lancaster entering service, the production rate was climbing (peaking at 155 aircraft per month in August 1944 by Avro alone), enabling 5 Group to re-equip ten squadrons, 1 Group with five squadrons and another with 3 Group. The newly formed 8 (Pathfinder Force) Group also initially operated two Lancaster squadrons, and it was the ambition of its AOC, AVM Don Bennett, to make his force an all-Lancaster and Mosquito affair as soon as was possible.

By the beginning of the Battle of the Ruhr, the number of available Lancasters continued to rise. During the first raid on Essen on 5/6 March 1943, the force of 442 aircraft included 157 Lancasters. The Ruhr campaign saw the Lancaster continue to feature as the most prolific bomber ahead of the Halifax and Stirling.

Both the Lancaster Mk I and Mk III would go on to form the backbone of Bomber Command, and at its peak 59 squadrons were equipped with the type; 56 of them were still in the front line in May 1945, with the ability to call up 1,000 aircraft at a moment's notice.

Production

There were 3,425 Lancaster Mk Is and 3,039 Mk IIIs built by Avro Ltd, Armstrong Whitworth Ltd, Austin Motors Ltd, Metropolitan-Vickers Ltd and Vickers-Armstrongs Ltd.

Technical data – 683 Lancaster Mk I & III	
ENGINE	(Proto) Four 1,145hp Rolls-Royce Merlin X; (Mk I) Four 1,280hp Merlin XX, 22 or 24; (Mk III) Four 1,300hp Packard Merlin 28, 1,480hp Packard Merlin 38 or 1,640hp Packard Merlin 224
WINGSPAN	102ft
LENGTH	69ft 4in
HEIGHT	20ft 6in
WING AREA	1,297 sq ft
TARE WEIGHT	36,457lb
ALL-UP WEIGHT	50,000lb
MAX SPEED	287mph
CRUISING SPEED	200mph
INITIAL CLIMB RATE	250ft/min
CEILING	19,000ft
RANGE	2,530 miles

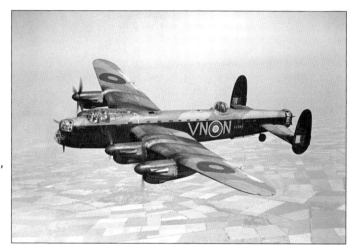

Right: Lancaster Mk I R5689 is seen during an air test from Woodford prior to delivery to 50 Squadron at Skellingthorpe. After moving to Swinderby, the bomber was lost on 19 September 1942 when two engines failed, forcing the Lancaster to crash land at Thurlby. (*Aeroplane*)

Below: The prototype Manchester Mk III, BT308 (officially renamed Lancaster by late January 1941) rests between test flights at Boscombe Down. Note the original Manchester type tail assembly including smaller fins and rudders. (Martyn Chorlton)

652A Anson Mk II to Mk X

Development

Despite attempts to send large numbers of Ansons to the Commonwealth, only a limited amount were getting through due to U-boat attacks and a shortage of Cheetah engines. As a result, it was found to be easier and more cost effective to begin production of the Anson outside Britain, and the main focus was on the industrial might of Canada.

Design

The first Anson variant to be built in Canada was the Mk II, which had modified windows and a plastic-bonded nose. Power was provided by a pair of Jacobs L-6MB R-915 engines, and the Mk II also introduced a single fork undercarriage, which could be retracted with a Dowty hydraulic system rather than being hand cranked like the Mk I.

The Mk V was an all-wooden version of the Anson introduced in an effort to save steel, with the fuselage entirely made of Vidal-moulded plywood. To retain the strength of the fuselage, the windows were changed to large portholes, three on each side, and the number of navigator trainees that could be carried was increased to five. Power was provided by a pair of 450hp Pratt & Whitney Wasp Junior engines, which drove Hamilton or Hoover constant-speed propellers. A single gunnery trainer, complete with a Bristol B.1 Mk VI turret, was also built and designated as the Anson Mk VI.

The Mk III, Mk IV and Mk X were all built in Britain by Avro; the former featuring 330hp L-6MB R-915 engines; the Mk IV 300hp Wright Whirlwind R-760-E1 radials and the latter 335hp Armstrong Siddeley Cheetah IXs. The Anson Mk X was a Mk I with a strengthened cabin floor, enabling it to carry heavy freight. The designations Mk VII, VIII and IX were reserved for Canadian variants but never taken up.

Service

The first Anson Mk II, 7069, a Mk I converted by Federal Aircraft Ltd made its maiden flight on 21 August 1941. This was followed in 1942 by the first Mk V, serialled 8649X, which was constructed from the major components of RCAF Mk I 6013 (ex-RAF N9943). The Mk V served the RCAF and the Royal Canadian Navy in a number of roles until 1954, when the last four in service were retired; three were sold onto the civilian market while the fourth, 12518, was preserved.

The Mk X entered RAF service from 1943, the majority serving with 24 and 353 squadrons, 4 and 5 AODU and the Air Transport Auxiliary (ATA); the type proving to be particularly useful in the light freight role, especially to the Continent following the D-Day invasion.

Production

There were 1,832 Mk IIs, 1,069 Mk Vs and a single Mk VI, all built in Canada by Canadian Car & Foundry Co. Ltd, de Havilland Aircraft of Canada Ltd, Federal Aircraft Ltd, MacDonald Brothers, National Steel Car Corporation, Ottawa Car and Aircraft Co. Ltd and Victory Aircraft. Out of this Canadian batch, 50 aircraft were supplied to the USAAF as AT-20s (43-8181 to 43-8230) with 330hp Jacobs R-915-7 engines. A further British-built 223 Mk III/IV manufactured at Avro's Newton Heath factory were supplied to Canada with Jacobs and Wright engines and 104 Mk Xs (converted from Mk Is) were built by Avro at Yeadon.

Technical data – Anson Mk II to Mk X	
ENGINE	(Mk II) Two 330hp Jacobs L6MB; (Mk V & VI) Two 450hp Pratt & Whitney Wasp Junior R985-AN12B or AN14B; (Mk X) Two 335hp Armstrong Siddeley Cheetah IX
WINGSPAN	56ft 6in
LENGTH	42ft 3in
HEIGHT	13ft 1in
WING AREA	463 sq ft
TARE WEIGHT	(Mk V & VI) 6,693lb
ALL-UP WEIGHT	(Mk V & VI) 9,460lb; (Mk X) 9,450lb
MAX SPEED	(Mk V & VI) 190mph; (Mk X) 175mph
CRUISING SPEED	(Mk V & VI) 145mph; (Mk X) 140mph
INITIAL CLIMB RATE	(Mk V & VI) 1,500ft/min
SERVICE CEILING	(Mk V & VI) 21,450ft
RANGE	(Mk V & VI) 580 miles

Right: **Avro Anson Mk V 12206 of the RCAF was built by MacDonald Brothers, Stevenson Field, Winnipeg, Canada. (Martyn Chorlton)**

Below: **Fifty Anson Mk IIs were supplied to the USAAF in 1943 and were redesignated AT-20. Of this batch, 39 were known to have been ex-RCAF aircraft. (Martyn Chorlton)**

683 Lancaster Mk II

Development

As demand for the Rolls-Royce Merlin engine increased for both fighters and bombers, alternative powerplants were considered for the Lancaster. To ensure that no potential interruption to Lancaster production took place, several hundred were fitted with the Bristol Hercules 14-cylinder air-cooled radial engine.

Design

The most obvious difference between the Mk II and all other Lancaster marks was the engines; initially 1,650hp Hercules VIs, which were later superseded by the Hercules XVI. The latter engine in particular gave the Lancaster similar performance figures to the Merlin-powered machines, although the service ceiling was restricted to just 18,500ft and fuel consumption was higher. One other difference between the Hercules and Merlin was that the former's Rotol propellers rotated to the left, while the latter's rotated to the right.

The Mk II also featured an extended bomb bay, which was first trialled on the second 'production' Lancaster prototype, DG585. This bomb bay was designed to accommodate the 5,500lb Capital Ship Bomb, but the weapon was aerodynamically unstable and virtually impossible to aim accurately resulting in it being abandoned later. The Mk II was also fitted with an aft facing FN.64 ventral gun turret, which had a field of fire of 100 degrees either side of the centreline.

Service

Two prototypes were ordered, DT810 and DT812, but the latter was cancelled as one was deemed sufficient; the aircraft first flying on 26 November 1941. The first of 300 production aircraft was delivered to Sywell in September 1942, followed by the first unit to receive the type, 61 Squadron at Syerston. 61 Squadron never became fully operational on the Mk II, but 115 Squadron at Witchford did when it began replacing its Wellington Mk IIIs from March 1943. 426 (Thunderbird) Squadron followed in July 1943, 514 Squadron in September and both 408 (Goose) and 432 (Leaside) squadrons in October. The type also served in small numbers with 1668 HCU at Balderton, 1679 HCU at

Technical data – 683 Lancaster Mk II	
ENGINE	Four 1,650hp Bristol Hercules VI or XVI
WINGSPAN	102ft
LENGTH	69ft 4in
HEIGHT	20ft 6in
WING AREA	1,297 sq ft
TARE WEIGHT	35,315lb
ALL-UP WEIGHT	60,000lb
MAX SPEED	270mph at 14,000ft
CEILING	18,500ft
RANGE	2,250 miles

East Moor and Wombleton and 1678 HCU at East Wretham, Little Snoring, Foulsham and finally Waterbeach. The latter unit was specifically formed to convert Wellington crews to the Lancaster Mk II and remained active until June 1944, when it was disbanded despite the bomber remaining operational with 408 (Goose) Squadron at Linton-on-Ouse until September 1944.

Production

There were 300 Lancaster Mk IIs all built by Armstrong Whitworth at Whitley, Coventry, for contract No.239/SAS/C4(C) between 1942 and 1943 and assembled at Baginton. Their serial ranges were DS601 to DS635, DS647 to DS692, DS704 to DS741, DS757 to DS797, DS813 to DS852, LL617 to LL652, LL666 to LL704 and LL716 to LL739, and all were delivered between September 1942 and March 1944.

The sole prototype Lancaster Mk II, DT810 is performing trials at Boscombe Down in September 1942. The aircraft performed much better than expected and the planned second prototype, DT812, was not built. (Martyn Chorlton)

A rare image of DS604 of 61 Squadron at Syerston, one of nine Mk IIs that served with the unit from January to March 1943, alongside the squadron's already established Lancaster Mk Is and Mk IIIs. All Mk IIs were transferred to 115 Squadron at Witchford. (Martyn Chorlton)

685 York C Mk 1 & C Mk 2

Development

The Avro York was one of several Lancaster derivatives that made full use of the original bomber's components, all grafted on to a new spacious fuselage. Although first flown in 1942, Britain's agreement with the US to concentrate on bomber and fighter production left manufacturers across the pond free to build new transport aircraft, and as a result the York was late to enter service, not reaching Transport Command until 1944 and then only in small numbers.

Design

The York was designed to an interim cargo specification numbered C.1/42, and to shorten development time the wings, engines, undercarriage and tail unit (production aircraft had an extra fin mounted on the fuselage) were taken from the Lancaster bomber. Internally, the York could be fitted out with passenger seats or as a freighter or a combination of the two. Designed by Roy Chadwick, the York had a new all-metal, square section fuselage with twice the cubic capacity of the Lancaster. Power was provided by four 1,620hp Merlin T.24 or 502 engines, although a single aircraft (the prototype LV626) was fitted with a quartet of 1,650hp Hercules VI engines to become the sole York C Mk 2.

Service

Prototype York C Mk 1 undertook its maiden flight from Ringway on 5 July 1942, but this aircraft did not enter RAF service with 24 Squadron at Hendon until March 1943. One of the unit's aircraft was the famous LV633, named *Ascalon*, which transported Winston Churchill to Algiers in May 1943 and King George VI on his tour of North Africa. Manufacturing of the York did not gain momentum until late 1943, when the first production aircraft were delivered to 511 Squadron at Lyneham in November. This unit, despite being briefly disbanded in October 1946, would operate the York for the longest continuous time until August 1949, when it was superseded by the Hastings.

By early 1948, nine RAF squadrons were operating the York, and all would be called upon to participate in Operation *Plainfaire*, aka the Berlin Airlift, together with the training unit, 241 Operational Conversion Unit (OCU). The Yorks made an invaluable contribution to the operation, flying 29,000 sorties and carrying 230,000 tons of supplies to the German capital: nearly half of the RAF's total contribution.

24 Squadron was the last unit to operate the York in March 1950, but one aircraft, MW295, named *Ascalon II*, continued to serve the FEAF Communications Squadron at Changi until 1957.

Operational RAF squadrons and service were 24 (March 1943 to October 1944 and July 1946 to December 1951), 40 (December 1947 to March 1950), 48 (one a/c MW173), 51 (January 1946 to October 1950), 59 (December 1947 to October 1950), 99 (November 1947 to September 1949), 206 (November 1947 to August 1949), 242 (April 1945 to July 1945 and December 1945 to September 1949), 246 (December 1944 to October 1946) and 511 Squadron (November 1943 to August 1949). The York also served with the RAF's 1332 HCU and 241 OCU as well as in limited numbers with the RAAF, SAAF and French Aéronavale.

Production

There were 203 Yorks delivered to the RAF from a total production of 257 aircraft. They were built in the serial ranges: MW100 to MW149, MW161 to MW210, MW223 to MW272, MW284 to MW333 and PE101 to PE108, all constructed at Woodford, Ringway and Yeadon.

Technical data – 685 York C Mk 1 & C Mk 2	
ENGINE	(Mk 1) Four 1,280hp Rolls-Royce Merlin 22 or 24; (Mk 2) Four Bristol Hercules XVI
WINGSPAN	102ft
LENGTH	78ft 6in
HEIGHT	17ft 10in
WING AREA	1,297 sq ft
TARE WEIGHT	42,040lb
ALL-UP WEIGHT	68,597lb
MAX SPEED	298mph at 21,000ft
CRUISING SPEED	233mph at 10,000ft
INITIAL CLIMB RATE	1,500ft/min
SERVICE CEILING	26,000ft
RANGE	2,700 miles

Right: The prototype York C Mk 1, LV626, is seen during early flight trials with the A&AEE at Boscombe Down during the late summer of 1942. (Martyn Chorlton)

Below: Hardworking York C Mk 1 MW248 at Northolt in early 1948. The aircraft served with 242, 206, 511 and 99 squadrons before it was lost on 4 July 1948, after colliding with a DC-6 on approach to Northolt. (*Aeroplane*)

683 Lancaster B Mk I & III 'Special'

Development

The Lancaster was ideally suited to carrying large single weapons, and its performance alone placed the bomber ahead of the Halifax and Stirling for the famous Dambusters Raid. Not a large weapon in its own right, the unusual shape of the Upkeep mine resulted in bomb bay modifications that would prove useful when the Tallboy and 10-ton Grand Slam weapons arrived from the summer of 1944.

Design

Although non-standard weapons, such as the 5,000lb Capital Ship bomb, had already been delivered by the Lancaster, the first device that required the aircraft to be modified was the Barnes Wallis-designed 9,250lb Upkeep mine (Vickers Type 464). The weapon was carried between a pair of large callipers, which released at exactly the same time for a clean release. To continue the bomb's clean trajectory and its skip across the water, the weapon was spun backwards ten minutes before being dropped by a Vickers Jassey hydraulic motor mounted on the starboard side of the mine. Power for this motor, which spun the bomb via a belt drive, was drawn from the same system that operated the mid-upper turret, which was removed. The Lancaster was also fitted with a pair of lights, forward and aft on the lower fuselage, their beams converging to become one when the correct delivery height of 60ft was achieved.

The next Wallis brainchild was the 12,000lb Tallboy bomb, an earthquake weapon designed to be dropped from 40,000ft. The bomb was 21ft long and 38in in diameter, but clever modification of the Lancaster's capacious bomb bay still meant that the weapon could be carried internally with an additional drop gear hitch. Special Stabilizing Automatic Bomb Sights (SABS) were fitted to each bomber.

The 22,000lb Grand Slam was 26ft 6in long and 3ft 10in across, which meant even the Lancaster would not be able to carry this devastating weapon internally. Extensive modifications would be needed, which included reducing defensive armament to a pair of machine guns in the rear turret. As with the Tallboy aircraft, better performing Merlin 24 engines were fitted. The bomb bay doors were completely removed, and the rear end was chopped to clear the tail of the weapon. The front end of the bomb bay was curved upwards to match the line of the front of the Grand Slam. Thirty-two aircraft were converted to carry the Grand Slam.

Service

Twenty-three aircraft were converted to carry the Upkeep, which was successfully employed for the unique operation carried out in May 1943 by 617 Squadron against the dams. The first of 700 Tallboys was dropped during a raid on a railway tunnel near Saumur on 8/9 June 1944, once again by 617 Squadron. The tunnel was blocked for the remainder of the war, and this crucially prevented the movement of a Panzer unit to the battle front. The first of 42 Grand Slam bombs was also delivered by 617 Squadron on 14 March 1945, when Sqn Ldr C. C. Calder attacked the viaduct at Bielefeld. The earthquake effect of the bomb reduced the central span to rubble, despite falling 100 yards away from the viaduct.

Technical data – 683 Lancaster B Mk I & Mk III 'Special'	
ENGINE	Four 1,280hp Rolls-Royce Merlin 22 or 24
WINGSPAN	102ft
LENGTH	69ft 4in
HEIGHT	20ft 6in
WING AREA	1,297 sq ft
TAKE-OFF WEIGHT	72,000lb with a 22,000lb Grand Slam
MAX SPEED	270mph
CRUISING SPEED	200mph
INITIAL CLIMB RATE	250ft/min
CEILING	25,000ft
RANGE	1,550 miles with a 22,000lb Grand Slam

Lancaster B Mk III (Special) ED817 of 617 Squadron was used for test dropping the Upkeep bouncing bomb during trials at Reculver. The aircraft was not actually used for the Dams Raid but the aircraft, bearing the code letter 'C' and flown by Plt Off W H T Ottley, failed to return from the operation. (Martyn Chorlton)

B Mk III (Special) PB995 was the first of 32 aircraft converted by Avro at Chadderton to carry the 22,000lb Grand Slam bomb, nicknamed 'ten-ton Tesse' in service. Allocated to the A&AEE for trials in February 1945, the aircraft was later transferred to 617 Squadron but never took part in operations. (Martyn Chorlton)

683 Lancaster Mk X

Development

As a nation, Canada had already contributed many aircrews and provided the RAF with extensive training facilities throughout the country. With a desire to contribute further, an agreement was reached with the Canadian government to build Lancasters under licence. In early 1942, the Victory Aircraft Company was formed at Malton, Ontario, and in August of that year, ex-44 Squadron Lancaster Mk I R5727 was sent to the company as a pattern aircraft. Conveniently, the Packard Company based at nearby Detroit, Michigan, just over 200 miles away, supplied Merlin 28, 38 and 224 engines for the new Lancaster, designated the Mk X. The first production Lancaster Mk X, KB700, left the Malton production line in September 1943, and the following month it arrived at Woodford in Cheshire for inspection by Avro.

All Lancasters produced by the Victory Aircraft Company were flown across the Atlantic to serve with RCAF squadrons. In total, 430 Lancaster Mk Xs were built in two blocks; the bulk of aircraft in the second did not see action, and many remained in RCAF service well into the 1950s and early 1960s.

Service

All Lancaster Mk Xs delivered to Britain were destined to serve with 6 (RCAF) Group operating from airfields in Yorkshire. Delivered to the UK from September 1943, the first production aircraft, KB700, was credited with joining 405 (Vancouver) Squadron at Linton-on-Ouse on 5 October 1943, but the unit did not take the Mk X on operations until May 1945. First to receive the Mk X in numbers was 419 (Moose) Squadron, based at Middleton St George, which began operations when nine Lancasters went into action in a raid on the railway yards at Montzen in Belgium on 27/28 April 1944. 428 (Ghost) Squadron began re-equipping from June 1944, 431 (Iroquois) from October, and 434 (Bluenose) Squadron from December. Four more units in 6 Group received the Mk X before the war was over, and after the Canadian squadrons returned home, all were disbanded in September 1945.

Technical data – 683 Lancaster Mk X	
ENGINE	Four 1,300hp Rolls-Royce Merlin 28, 1,480hp Merlin 38 or 1,640hp Merlin 224
WINGSPAN	102ft
LENGTH	69ft 4in
HEIGHT	20ft 6in
WING AREA	1,297 sq ft
TARE WEIGHT	36,457lb
ALL-UP WEIGHT	68,000lb
MAX SPEED	287mph
CRUISING SPEED	200mph
INITIAL CLIMB RATE	250ft/min
CEILING	19,000ft
RANGE	2,530 miles

Post-war, the Mk X served on with the RCAF in a number of guises including the 10-AR (area recce variant); 10-BR (bomber recce); 10-DC (target drone carrier); 10-MR/MP (maritime recce and later maritime patrol); 10-N (flying classroom for navigators); 10-O (Orenda test bed) and 10-P (photo recce and mapping). In RCAF service, the last of Lancaster Mk X derivatives was not retired until 1 April 1964.

Production

There were 430 Lancaster Mk Xs built in two batches, beginning with 300 delivered by Victory Aircraft between September 1943 and March 1945, in the serial range KB700 to KB999. The second batch was for 200 aircraft, but only 130 were built, again by Victory Aircraft, which delivered them between April and August 1945 in the serial range FM100 to FM299.

Right: **FM207 was the very last Lancaster Mk X to be delivered to Britain on 22 August 1945, only to return to Canada in November. Allocated to 408 Squadron RCAF, the aircraft was converted into a Mk 10-P in 1952 and continued to serve for almost a decade in this form. (Martyn Chorlton)**

Below: **FM211 was placed into storage immediately after the end of the war but was later converted into a Mk 10-MR. The aircraft served with the RCAF's CFS and was named *Zenith*, serving until late 1955. (Martyn Chorlton)**

683 Lancaster Mk VI & VII (B.7)

Development

Efforts to increase the performance of the standard Lancaster Mk III failed to fully materialise in the Mk VI, and the continued need for more firepower came too late for service during World War Two in the Mk VII. However, the latter was produced in healthy numbers, and during the immediate post-war period saw service with five operational squadrons, and the Mk VI would prove to be a useful engine test bed.

Design

The Lancaster Mk VI was the result of a proposal to improve the performance of the Mk III by installing a quartet of 1,750hp Merlin 85 engines. Two Mk IIIs, DV170 and DV199, were despatched to Rolls-Royce at Hucknall on 16 June and 6 July 1943, respectively, for conversion. A further seven Mk IIIs were converted to Mk VI standard for service trials, several examples going on to serve with 8 Group as part of 635 Squadron complete with a faired-over forward turret and no dorsal turret. Maximum speed of the Mk VI was 313mph at 18,000ft, but one aircraft, ND558, achieved the Lancaster record when it reached 350mph (Mach 0.72) in a dive during tests at Boscombe Down.

The Mk VII differed from all other variants by its dorsal turret, which was an American-built electrically powered Martin furnished with a pair of 0.5in Browning machine guns. The turret was positioned over the rear bomb bay, which was further forward than the original Frazer-Nash turret. Post-war, the bomber was referred to as the B.7, and a tropicalised version was designated as the B.7 (FE). The 'Far East' variant was to have formed the backbone of the RAF's 'Tiger Force' against the Japanese, but thankfully the war ended before the type saw action.

Service

The first Lancaster Mk VI, DV170, was flying by August 1943, and along with the second and third prototypes, DV199 and JB675, all focused on Merlin development. The remainder were allocated for service trials, examples briefly serving with 7, 83, 106, 405 and 582 squadrons. Five aircraft, JB675, JB713, ND418, ND558 and ND673, did serve operationally with 635 Squadron between July and November 1944; JB713 failed to return from Harburg on 18/19 August 1944.

The Lancaster Mk VII (FE) first entered service with 617 Squadron in June 1945 at Waddington, in preparation for a five-month tour to Digri, 65 miles west of Calcutta, in January 1946. The mark also served with 9 (November 1945 to April 1946), 37 (June 1946 to March 1947), 40 (January 1946 to March 1947) and 104 squadrons ([FE] November 1945 to March 1947).

Production

Only nine Mk VIs were converted from Mk IIIs: DV170, DV199, JB675, JB713, ND418, ND479, ND558, ND673 and ND784.

Mk VII production entailed an initial batch of 30 aircraft built by Austin Motors Ltd, serialled RT670 to RT699, delivered between November 1945 and December 1946; a second batch of 40 aircraft was cancelled. A third batch of 150 aircraft, also built by Austin Motors Ltd, serialled NX611 to NX648, NX661 to NX703, NX715 to NX758 and NX770 to NX794 were delivered between April and September 1945.

Technical data – 683 Lancaster Mk VI & Mk VII	
ENGINE	(Mk VI) Four 1,750hp Rolls-Royce Merlin 85, 87 or 102; (Mk VI also trialled) Merlin series 65, 85, 100, 102 and 621; (Mk VII) Four 1,620hp Merlin 24
WINGSPAN	102ft
LENGTH	69ft 4in
HEIGHT	20ft 6in
WING AREA	1,297 sq ft
ALL-UP WEIGHT	(Mk VII) 68,000lb
MAX SPEED	(Mk VI) 313mph at 18,200ft; (Mk VII) 275mph

Delivered to Rolls-Royce at Hucknall as a standard Mk III on 16 June 1943, DV170 re-emerged a few weeks later as a Merlin 85-powered Mk VI. The aircraft remained as a Merlin test bed and here is fitted with four Merlin 102 engines developed for the Avro Tudor. (Martyn Chorlton)

A Lancaster Mk VII. (Key Archives)

652A Anson Mk 11 & 12

Development

Despite having entered service in the mid-1930s the Avro Anson continued to evolve, and one of the most significant design changes took place in 1944 with the introduction of the Mk 11 and Mk 12 (later referred to as the C.11 and C.12).

Design

The appearance of the Anson was changed slightly by the introduction of the Mk 11 due to a redesigned raised cabin, which gave the crew considerably more headroom. The original extensive glazing along each side of the fuselage was replaced with much neater square windows. Both the flaps and the undercarriage were also hydraulically operated, as per the Canadian-built Mk II. Later production versions of the Mk 12 were fitted with metal wings, and these were designated as the Mk 12 Series 2. Several examples of both marks were also converted to air ambulances, modified with hinged root fillets on the port side of fuselage to allow for stretchers.

The Mk 11 was powered by two 395hp Cheetah XIX engines driving Fairey-Reed fixed pitch metal propellers while the Mk 12 had a pair of 420hp Cheetah XVs fitted with Rotol constant-speed propellers.

Service

The first Anson Mk 11, NK790 undertook its maiden flight in May 1944, followed by the first ambulance version, NK870, on 30 July. The prototype Mk 12 was first flown from Woodford on 5 September 1944, by which time production of the earlier mark was in full swing.

Both marks served with an array of communication, command, group and station flights during their careers, which continued into the late 1950s. In squadron service, the Mk 11/C.11 only served with 58 Squadron from October 1946 until July 1947, after the unit had been reformed at Benson. The Mk 12/C.12 saw more widespread use beginning with 147 Squadron at Croydon from September 1944 to September 1945. The aircraft also served with 31 (July 1948 to March 1955), 116 (March 1945 to May 1945), 147 (September 1944 to September 1945), 167 (April 1945 to February 1946) and 187 squadrons (April 1955 to September 1957).

Production

Ninety Mk 11s (originally laid down as Mk Is) were built at Yeadon in the serial ranges NK790, NK870 to NK875, NK940, NK986 to NK999, NL125, NL128, NL129, NL132, NL133, NL136, NL137, NL140, NL141, NL144, NL145, NL148, NL149, NL181 to NL208 and NL220 to NL246.

The first batch of Mk 12s (originally laid down as Mk Is) were built at Yeadon with the serials MG159, NK150, NK151, NL152, NL153, NL171, NL172, NL175, NL176, NL179, NL180 and NL247 to NL251. The second batch of Mk 12s built new comprised 255 aircraft, again constructed at Yeadon in the serial ranges PH528 to PH569, PH582 to PH626, PH638 to PH679, PH691 to PH735, PH747 to PH789 and PH803 to PH840.

Technical data – 652A Anson Mk 11 & 12	
ENGINE	(Mk 11) Two 395hp Armstrong Siddeley Cheetah 19; (Mk 12) Two 420hp Cheetah 15
WINGSPAN	56ft 6in
LENGTH	42ft 3in
HEIGHT	13ft 10in
WING AREA	463 sq ft
TARE WEIGHT	7,419lb
ALL-UP WEIGHT	(Mk 11) 9,700lb; (Mk 12) 10,500lb
MAX SPEED	190mph
CRUISING SPEED	167mph
INITIAL CLIMB RATE	730ft/min
CEILING	15,000ft
RANGE	610 miles

The first production/prototype Mk 11, NK790 is seen prior to its maiden flight in May 1944. In typical Anson fashion, the aircraft went on to serve with a variety of units and manufacturers, including the RAE, Helliwells, Aircraft Torpedo Development Unit (ATDU), British Messier and the Bombing Trials Unit (BTU) before being sold on the civilian market on 10 March 1955. (Martyn Chorlton)

694 Lincoln B Mk 1 to 4 & Mk 30B

Development

In late 1941, when the Japanese entered the war and quickly advanced across the Far East, the sudden realisation reared itself in the shape of a distinct lack of aircraft carriers and long-range bombers in the British and Commonwealth military inventories. Acquiring large numbers of B-24 Liberators was the only realistic short-term solution, but they lacked the bombload at the extremes of their range. The long-term answer was to design a new aircraft or modify an existing one, and discussions on this subject began between the Air Ministry and Roy Chadwick in 1942.

Design

While other manufacturers considered a completely new aircraft, unlikely to be in service by the late 1940s, let alone before the end of the war, Avro looked at upgrading the Lancaster. Designed to specification B.14/43, the aircraft was original called the Lancaster Mk IV and Mk V, but modifications were so extensive it became a new type, called the Lincoln. Still utilising almost 80 per cent of the Lancaster's original structure, the Lincoln had higher aspect ratio wings, a longer fuselage and more powerful Merlin engines (the specification called for a Griffon or Centaurus, however these would never become available). The Lincoln B Mk 2 was powered by Packard-built engines while the B Mk 4 was re-engined with the original Merlin 85 engines. The Mk 4s were also equipped with electronic jamming equipment for service with Signals Command.

Service

Pressure to build more Lancasters delayed the maiden flight of the prototype until 9 June 1944. Consequently, the Lincoln B Mk 1 did not enter operational service until August 1945 with 57 Squadron at East Kirkby as part of the Tiger Force. By the end of 1945, 57 Squadron had been disbanded, their aircraft being transferred to 103 Squadron, joined later in the year by 44 Squadron. B Mk 2s, the main variant, later served with 7, 9, 12, 15, 35, 44, 49, 50, 57, 58, 61, 75, 83, 90, 97, 100, 101, 115, 138, 148, 149, 207, 214 and 617 squadrons into the mid-1950s, the majority being replaced by the Canberra.

The Mk 4s served on with the electronic countermeasure (ECM) units, 116, 192, 199 and 527 squadrons, although it was the radar development aircraft of 151 Squadron at Watton that brought the Lincolns RAF service to an end in May 1963. Licence-built Lincolns also served with the RAAF from 1946 through to 1961, and the Argentine Air Force operated 30 examples from 1947 to 1967.

Production

Three Lincoln prototypes, serialled PW925, PW929 and PW932, were followed by a contract for 162 aircraft to be built by Avro, plus a further six aircraft made up of B Mk 1s. Sixty-nine B Mk 1s and Mk 2s were built by Metropolitan-Vickers and 281 aircraft were constructed by Armstrong Whitworth, of which 200 were B Mk 2s. Sixty of these B Mk 2s later modified to Mk 4 standard. The Australian Government Aircraft Factory built 24 Mk.30(B), 30 Mk.30A(B) and carried 18 conversions to Mk.31(MR) standard. Eighteen aircraft, originally built by Armstrong Whitworth, were diverted to Avro for the Argentine Air Force, and a further 12 were reconditioned for the same purpose by Short Brothers and Harland Ltd in Belfast.

Technical data – 694 Lincoln B Mk 1	
ENGINE	(B Mk 1 & Mk 4) Four 1,680hp Rolls-Royce Merlin 85; (B Mk 2) four Packard Merlin 66, 68 and 300; (B Mk 15) four 1,750hp Merlin 68A; (Mk.30B) four 1,750hp Merlin 85 or 102
WINGSPAN	120ft
LENGTH	78ft 3½in
HEIGHT	17ft 3½in
WING AREA	1,421 sq ft
EMPTY WEIGHT	(B Mk 1) 43,778lb; (B Mk 2) 44,148lb
LOADED WEIGHT	82,000lb
MAX SPEED	295mph at 15,000ft
CRUISING SPEED	238mph at 15,000ft
CLIMB RATE	820ft/min; 26½mins to 20,000ft
SERVICE CEILING	23,000ft
RANGE	1,470 miles with a 14,000lb bomb load; 2,930 miles with a full fuel load

Right: A pair of 148 Squadron's Lincolns tail chase out of RAF Upwood, heading north over the village of Ramsey St Mary's. RE397, in the lead, served solely with 148 Squadron until 5 September 1953, when it was written off at Wittering after the undercarriage collapsed on take-off. (*Aeroplane*)

Below: Avro Lincoln Mk.30s of 1 Squadron RAAF at Tengah during the Malayan Emergency, which lasted from 1948 to 1960. (*Aeroplane*)

683 Lancaster Test Beds

The engine test beds
The Lancaster proved to be a reliable test bed for a wide range of engine development encompassing the most powerful versions of the Merlin, early turboprops and jets from 1943 through to the mid-1950s.

The aircraft (in serial order)
R5849: Mk I delivered direct to Rolls-Royce at Hucknall on 24 April 1942 to trial the 1,700hp Merlin 600 engine with annular cowlings. The aircraft caught fire on final approach to Hucknall on 11 June 1943 and was burnt out on the ground after the crew managed to escape.

BT308: The Lancaster prototype BT308 was delivered to Rolls-Royce on 28 February 1942 to test a Metropolitan-Vickers F.2 axial-flow gas-turbine in the rear fuselage.

JB675: Laid down as a Mk III, JB675 was converted to a Mk IV and delivered to Rolls-Royce in November 1943. Here, the aircraft was installed with a pair of 1,770hp Merlin 621s, planned for the Tudor Mk I, inboard, and a pair of 1,760hp Merlin 621s, planned for the Canadair C-4, outboard. The aircraft was scrapped in July 1948.

LL735: An Armstrong Whitworth-built Mk II, LL735 was delivered to Rolls-Royce to continue trials with the F.2 gas-turbine following the loss of BT308. The F.2/1 was first flown on 29 June 1943 and later also trialled the 3,500lb F.2/4 Beryl in 1945. The aircraft was scrapped in 1950.

ND784: Another Mk III converted to Mk IV standard, ND784/G was initially delivered to Rolls-Royce at Hucknall and then to Power Jets Ltd at Bruntingthorpe on 11 October 1944. Prior to this, the aircraft briefly served with the RAE where it was known as the 'Lancaster Universal Test Bed'. Engine configurations included four Merlin XXs and a 2,600lb Armstrong Siddeley ASX in the bomb bay and later four 1,750hp Merlin 85s and an Armstrong Siddeley Mamba in the nose.

NG465: This Mk I saw active service with 90, 186 and 218 squadrons before it was transferred to Rolls-Royce at Hucknall in August 1946. The aircraft was used to test a 1,000hp Dart engine in the nose from October 1947 and was also modified to carry a pair of 100-gallon water tanks in the rear fuselage for icing trials. Several Dart turboprops were trialled before the aircraft was written off in a forced landing near Mansfield on 22 January 1954.

PP791: Delivered to Rolls-Royce, Hucknall, as a general test bed; trials included the 1,770hp Merlin 600 engine.

RE137: Having served with 514 Squadron, Mk III RE137 served with the National Gas Turbine Establishment and Armstrong Siddeley Motors at Baginton from 1947. The aircraft was used to trial a pair of 3,670hp Python propeller-turbines fitted with eight blade contra-rotating propellers in the outboard positions.

SW342: Yeadon-built Mk III SW342 was modified by Air Service Training at Hamble in January 1949 to trial a nose-mounted Mamba propeller-turbine. Icing trials were conducted from Bitteswell, and in

May 1952 the aircraft flew with four 1,640hp Merlin 24s, a Mamba with a cropped airscrew in the nose, surrounded by an icing rig and an Adder turbojet in the tail. The aircraft was scrapped in 1956.

TW911: Mk I (FE) TW911 was delivered to Armstrong Siddeley in March 1946, and on 3 January 1949, it flew with a pair of 1,610hp Merlin 24s inboard and two 3,670hp Python I propeller-turbines outboard. The aircraft was SOC in January 1953.

FM205: A Mk X modified by Avro (Canada) to test a pair of 3,000lb Avro Chinook T.R.4 engines outboard, but the engines never flew. Possibly used for Orenda testing instead in 1951.

FM209: A Mk X, converted the same as FM205 for Orenda testing in the outboard nacelles.

80001: Aircraft bought new for the Swedish Air Force and converted by Air Service Training to test a 7,360lb Stal Dorven turbojet in a ventral pod. It also tested a Ghost with reheat for the SAAB J29, but it crashed on 8 May 1956.

Technical data – 683 Lancaster test beds	
ENGINES	(all aircraft) Four 1,770hp Rolls-Royce Merlin 600, 1,770hp Merlin 621, 1,760hp Merlin 620, Merlin XX, 1,750hp Merlin 85, 1,610hp and 1,640hp Merlin 24; Metropolitan-Vickers F.2 and F.2/1; 3,500lb F.2/4 Beryl; 2,600lb Armstrong Siddeley ASX; Armstrong Siddeley Mamba; 1,000hp plus 325lb st Rolls-Royce Dart No.3, No.5, No.15 and No.15; 3,670hp Armstrong Siddeley Python and Python I; Adder turbojet; 7,360lb Stal Dorven; Rolls-Royce Ghost; Avro Canada Orenda

Lancaster Mk III SW342 is fully tooled up with the Mamba, complete with icing rig in the nose, four Merlin 24s and an Adder turbojet in the rear fuselage. Note the Mamba's cropped airscrew within the icing rig. (*Aeroplane*)

Called the 'Lancaster Universal Test Bed' because of the wide range of powerplants it tested, the aircraft is pictured with an Armstrong Siddeley Mamba in the nose. (Martyn Chorlton)

652A Anson Mk 18 to 22

Development

The incredible story of the Anson came to a conclusion with the production of the final marks – the Mk 18 through to Mk 22. Production reached 11,020 when the last example, a T Mk 21, left the Yeadon factory on 27 May 1952. These final examples would continue to serve the RAF through to the type's retirement in 1968, bringing to an end a service career spanning over three decades.

Design

The metal-winged Anson Mk 18 was built specifically for the Afghan government and was furnished for liaison, policing, transport and survey duties. The Mk 19 was a more significant variant, the military version being a development of the civil Avro 19 series. Very similar to the Mk XII, the aircraft, designated the C Mk 19 in RAF service, had improved internal trim, better cabin sound-proofing and oval windows instead of the earlier square type. Twenty C Mk 19s were converted from Mk XIIs, while the bulk of the production aircraft were designated as Series 2s, because they had metal wings and tailplanes.

The first of three trainer variants, the T Mk 20, designed to specification T.24/46 featured a transparent nose for a bomb-aimer. The final two variants, the T Mk 21 (T.25/46) and T Mk 22 (T.26/46), were built as navigation and radio trainers, respectively.

Service

The C Mk 19 first entered operational service with 147 Squadron at Croydon in April 1946 and would go on to serve with a wide range of units in the communications and transport roles. The T Mk 20 was used as a navigation and wireless operator trainer in RAF service. There was sufficient room in the aircraft for a single wireless operator trainee and an instructor, and there were a further five stations for three trainee navigators and a pair of instructors. The type saw extensive service in Southern Rhodesia as a bombing and navigation trainer.

The T Mk 21 predominantly served the RAF within Flying Training Command, although the type also served with 228 (September 1959 to March 1960) and 275 (July 1954 to September 1959) squadrons, both Air-Sea Rescue units at the time. The T Mk 22s all served as radio trainers for air signallers. The Mk 18 for the Royal Afghan Air Force served from 1948 through to 1956.

The Anson remained in RAF service until 28 June 1968, when the final six serviceable aircraft, five C Mk 19s and a T Mk 21 all serving with the Southern Communication Squadron based at Bovingdon, conducted a formation flypast to mark the type's official retirement.

Production

The Mk 18 prototype VP151 plus 13 aircraft were built for the Afghan government; C Mk 19 prototype PH806, plus 296 production aircraft were built in the serial prefixes PJ, TX, VL, VM and VP; T Mk 20, prototype VM305, plus 59 built in the serial ranges VM410 to VM418, VS491 to VS561 and VS866 and VS867; T Mk 21 prototype VS562 was first flown in May 1948, and 252 production aircraft were built in the serial ranges VS562 to VS591, VV239 to VV999, WB446 to WB465, WD402 to WD418 and WJ509 to WJ561; T Mk 22 prototype VM306, plus 33 were built aircraft in the serial ranges VS592 to VS603, VV358 to VV370 and WD419 to WD436.

Technical data – Anson Mk 18, C Mk 19, T Mk 20, T Mk 21 & T Mk 22	
ENGINE	(Mk 18) Two 420hp Armstrong Cheetah 17; (All other marks) 420hp Cheetah 15
WINGSPAN	57ft 6in
LENGTH	42ft 3in
HEIGHT	13ft 10in
WING AREA	440 sq ft
TARE WEIGHT	6,576lb
ALL-UP WEIGHT	10,400lb; (T Mk 22) 10,306lb
MAX SPEED	171mph
CRUISING SPEED	149mph
INITIAL CLIMB RATE	700ft/min
CEILING	16,000ft
RANGE	660 miles

Avro chief test pilot Jimmy Orrell leans forward in his seat to keep an eye on the photo aircraft during the test flight of T Mk 21 WJ561 on 15 May 1952. The last of the 11,020 Ansons built, the aircraft is aloft over Woodford during this historic flight. (Martyn Chorlton)

688 Tudor Mk 8

Development

Ordered by the Ministry of Supply, and jointly built by Avro and the Rolls-Royce Research and Development Department at Hucknall, the Avro Tudor Mk 8 was one of the pioneering jet-powered aircraft of the post-war period.

Design

The second Tudor Mk I airframe, TT181, was selected for conversion to jet-power in early 1948, by which time the aircraft had already been upgraded to Mk 4 standard, complete with forward fuselage extension and had also been allocated the civilian registration G-AGST.

Redesignated as the Mk 8, the aircraft was fitted with four Rolls-Royce Nene 4 turbojets, each producing 5,000lb of static thrust. The fitment of the powerplant, design of the engine nacelles and the main undercarriage assemblies were all the responsibility of Rolls-Royce. The latter neatly retracted between the jet pipes, which were fed air via a bifurcated intake, while thrust exited to the rear of the trailing edge through a pair of comparatively widely spaced tail pipes. The Tudor's tail-dragger undercarriage arrangement was retained, which, combined with the low-slung position of the engines, would prove to be the type's only major design fault. Publicly demonstrated at Farnborough, when the throttles were opened the jet efflux quickly heated the tarmac runway, causing great clouds of unsightly smoke.

Internally, the spacious Tudor cabin was fully exploited for a variety of test equipment, which would prove beneficial to both the military and civilian aviation industry.

Service

Re-serialled VX195, the Tudor Mk 8 was first flown by Jimmy Orrell from Woodford on 6 September1948, and just three days later the aircraft made its first public appearance at the SBAC, Farnborough. After being demonstrated by Orrell at the show, the aircraft returned to Woodford on 13 September, where the Tudor was thoroughly checked over before being transferred to the A&AEE at Boscombe Down on 25 October for performance and calibration trials, which came to an end on 10 November.

Pilots lucky enough to fly the Tudor Mk 8 were all complimentary with regard to the aircraft's handling and performance. Special mention was made about the peace and comfort in the cockpit compared to the cluttered and noisy environment of a piston-powered machine.

VX195 returned to Boscombe Down in September 1949 for further trials, remaining in military hands as the aircraft was later transferred to the RAE at Farnborough. Dismantled by 1951, the fuselage lived on for a while in the hands of Teddington Controls Ltd, who used it as a static rig pressurisation chamber into the early 1950s.

The Ministry of Supply placed a further order for six aircraft designated the Tudor Mk 9, which was based on the Tudor Mk 2 complete with a tricycle undercarriage. These materialised as the 706 Ashton.

Technical data – 688 Tudor Mk 8	
ENGINE	Four 5,000lb Rolls-Royce Nene 5
WINGSPAN	120ft
LENGTH	79ft 3in
HEIGHT	20ft 11in
WING AREA	1,421 sq ft
TARE WEIGHT	34,724lb
ALL-UP WEIGHT	80,000lb
MAX SPEED	385mph
CRUISING SPEED	350mph
INITIAL CLIMB RATE	2,930ft/min
CEILING	44,000ft
RANGE	1,720 miles

The best looking of the Tudor family by far, the Nene-powered Mk 8 had a short but productive career as a research and development aircraft between 1948 and 1950. (Martyn Chorlton)

701 Athena
T Mk 1 & T Mk 2

Development

The Avro Athena was built to specification T.7/45 calling for a Harvard and, to a lesser extent, a Prentice replacement, both serving as the RAF standard basic trainer. In competition with the Boulton Paul Balliol, the Athena was a turbine-powered three-seater, although the few aircraft that were built entered RAF service with a traditional Merlin engine.

Design

Work began on the all-metal Athena T Mk 1, designed by S. D. Davies in March 1947. The aircraft was a low-wing monoplane that made use of the same aerofoil employed by the Hawker Tempest, so that the trainer would handle like a fighter. Only three T Mk 1s were destined to be built, two of them were powered by the Armstrong Siddeley Mamba, while the third, designated T Mk 1A, was powered by a Rolls-Royce Dart I turboprop. The reason for this was because the Air Ministry moved the goal posts with their requirement for Flying Training Command, coupled with a shortage of turbine engines. Plentiful stocks of Merlin engines were available, and as result specification T.14/17 was issued, stipulating the use of this powerplant. The turbine-powered Athenas performed well, and the small powerplant gave a good view over the nose for the crew.

The result was the Athena T Mk 2, powered by a Merlin 35 engine; a much heavier engine that forced the position of the mainplane forward by 27 inches to compensate for the weight. Cooling was provided by a large beard-type Morris radiator directly below the Merlin. The strongly built Athena was designed to take a lot of punishment and in theory could be landed wheels-up without causing serious damage to the airframe. The central section of the T Mk 2 incorporated a Lockheed undercarriage, fuel tanks, a .303in Browning machine gun (with 300 rounds of ammunition) and G.45 gun camera. The Athena was also fitted with hardpoints for either 45-gallon drop tanks or bomb racks, and a target-towing point was located under the tail.

Service

The first of three T Mk 1 prototypes, VM125, powered by a Mamba turboprop, was initially flown from Woodford by Jimmy Orrell on 12 June 1948. The first T Mk 2, VW890, followed on 1 August 1948, and after evaluation at Boscombe Down and modifications, which included an increased area fin, the first Athenas, VR566 and VR567, joined the CFE in October 1949. The few T Mk 2s built found a useful role as an armament trainer, replacing the Harvard, with the RAF Flying College at Manby from 1950 to 1955, where the aircraft's useful hardpoints were used to carry a pair of 60lb rocket projectiles.

Production

Three T Mk 1 prototypes, VM125 (Mamba), VM129 (Dart) and VM132 (Mamba) were built, followed by T Mk 2 prototypes VW890 to VW893. Fifteen production aircraft, built to contract 6/ACFT/174 and serialled VR566 to VR580, were delivered between October 1949 and September 1951. VR563 to VR565 and VR581 and VR582 were all cancelled.

Technical data – 701 Athena T Mk 1 & T Mk 2	
ENGINE	(T Mk 1) One 1,010hp Armstrong Siddeley Mamba I; (T Mk 1A) One 1,400hp Rolls-Royce Dart I; (T Mk 2) One 1,280hp Rolls-Royce Merlin 35
WINGSPAN	40ft
LENGTH	(T Mk 1) 36ft 6in; (T Mk 2) 37ft 3½in
HEIGHT	(T Mk 1) 11ft 11in; (T Mk 2) 12ft 11in
WING AREA	270 sq ft
EMPTY WEIGHT	(T Mk 1 Mamba) 5,067lb; (T Mk 2) 6,540lb
LOADED WEIGHT	(T Mk 1 Mamba) 7,191lb; (T Mk 2) between 9,043 and 9,383lb
MAX SPEED	(T Mk 1 Mamba) 291mph at 20,000ft; (T Mk 2) 293 at 20,000ft
CRUISING SPEED	(T Mk 1 Mamba) 256mph; (T Mk 2) 223mph
INITIAL CLIMB RATE	(T Mk 1 Mamba) 2,640ft/min; (T Mk 2) 2,050ft/min
SERVICE CEILING	(T Mk 1 Mamba) 34,800ft; (T Mk 2) 29,000ft
RANGE	(T Mk 1 Mamba) 620 miles; (T Mk 2) 550 miles

Right: The second production Avro Athena T Mk 2, VR567 is in service with the CFS at Little Rissington circa early 1950. (Martyn Chorlton)

Below: VR569 was registered as G-ALWA in February 1950 for a demonstration tour in India and is seen here at Farnborough in September, after reverting to its military serial, when demonstrated by Jimmy Nelson. While being trialled with the Armament & Instrument Experimental Unit at Martlesham Heath, the aircraft crashed on 27 June 1951, killing Fg Off J R Corke and Sgt J E A Walsh; the only Athena fatalities during its five years of service. (Martyn Chorlton)

696 Shackleton MR Mk 1 & T Mk 4

Development

The capability the Liberator and Fortress had provided for the RAF's Coastal Command during World War Two was not abandoned during the post-war period, but these lend-lease machines would need replacing with a British-built aircraft.

Design

A development of the Lincoln Mk III, a projected anti-submarine version of the bomber that never left the drawing board, the new aircraft drew heavily from both Tudor and Lincoln components. Designed to Air Ministry specification R.5/36 the new aircraft, named the Shackleton, used the wings and undercarriage from a Lincoln plus the tail plane unit, although this was repositioned higher on the rear fuselage. The stress-skinned fuselage was completely redesigned with much more internal space than the Lincoln, while power was provided by Griffon engines driving six-bladed contra-rotating propellers.

The prototypes were initially designated as the GR Mk 1 (General Reconnaissance); this was later changed to the MR Mk 1 (Maritime Reconnaissance). A sub-variant, the MR Mk 1A, differed by its engines, which were all Griffon 57A, whereas the Mk 1 was fitted with these engines in the inboard position and Griffon 57s in the outboard. The T Mk 4 was stripped of all defensive armament and was internally modified with extra radar stations for both pupils and instructors.

Armament of the MR Mk 1 and Mk 1A was a 20mm Hispano cannon either side of the nose, two more in a Bristol B.27 mid-upper turret and a pair of 0.5in machine guns in the tail. Offensive weapons included depth charges and a wide range of bombs, all managed by a crew of ten. A distinctive feature that was unique to the Shackleton MR Mk 1 and Mk 1A was a prominent radome under the chin, which housed an ASV scanner.

Technical data – 696 Shackleton MR Mk 1, Mk 1A & T Mk 4	
ENGINE	(MR Mk 1 & T Mk 4) Two 2,450hp Rolls-Royce Griffon 57 and two Griffon 57A; (MR Mk 1A & T Mk 4) four 2,450hp Griffon 57A
WINGSPAN	120ft
LENGTH	87ft 3in
HEIGHT	16ft 9in
WING AREA	1,421 sq ft
EMPTY WEIGHT	54,200lb
LOADED WEIGHT	86,000lb
MAX SPEED	300mph at 18,300ft
SERVICE CEILING	25,700ft
RANGE	3,800 miles at 200mph

Service

The prototype, VW126, was first flown by Jimmy Orrell from Woodford on 9 March 1949 followed by the first production aircraft, VP254, on 24 October 1950. Entry into service came in February 1951, when the type simultaneously joined 236 OCU and 120 Squadron, both stationed at Kinloss; the latter until October 1956. The Mk 1 also served with 42 (June 1952 to July 1954), 203 (November 1958 to February 1959), 204 (May 1958 to February 1960), 205 (May 1958 to September 1962), 206 (September 1952 to May 1958), 220 (September 1951 to February 1958), 224 (July 1951 to August 1954), 240 (May 1952 to November 1958) and 269 squadrons (January 1952 to November 1958), the type replacing the Sunderland GR Mk 5 and Halifax GR Mk 6 in the maritime role, although the bulk of these units were re-formed with the Shackleton.

The Shackleton MR Mk 1 and Mk 1A remained in service longer than planned and were operated alongside its intended replacement, the MR Mk 2, for many years and were not withdrawn until September 1962.

Production

Three prototypes, VW126, VW131 and VW135 were built, followed by 29 production MR Mk 1s, serialled VP254 to VP268 and VP281 to VP294, and 48 production MR Mk 1As, serialled WB818 to WB837, WB844 to WB861, WG507 to WG511 and WG525 to WG529. Seventeen aircraft were converted from Mk 1As to T Mk 4 standard, serialled VP258, VP259, VP293, WB819, WB820, WB822, WB826, WB831, WB832, WB837, WB844, WB845, WB847, WB849, WB858, WG511 and WG527.

A 269 Squadron Shackleton poses for the camera east of Dunluce Castle on the dramatic North Antrim coast. Re-formed at Gibraltar from 224 Squadron on 1 January 1952, the unit moved to Ballykelly on 24 March 1952 with its Shackleton MR Mk 1s, which it retained until November 1958. (*Aeroplane*)

707, A, B & C

Development

It was not unusual for a pre-prototype or two to be built when a revolutionary design that stretched the aerodynamic knowledge of the day was on the table. However, when Avro presented its ground-breaking design for a delta winged bomber of never-before-seen proportions, further research would definitely be needed. This research could only be conducted by a special test aircraft, which would eventually lead to five different airframes spread over four different marks. This aircraft was the Avro 707, the first British-built delta.

Design

Work began on the first 707 in mid-1948 under the specification E.15/48. A simple design, the aircraft made use of a large number of components from other aircraft. These included the canopy and nose wheel arrangement from a Meteor and the main undercarriage from an Athena. The 707 was powered by a Derwent 5, which, unusually, was fed air via a bifurcated dorsal intake set behind the cockpit, upsetting the lines of an otherwise attractive little aircraft.

The 707B, the second aircraft to be built, featured a wing with 51-degree leading edge sweepback while the 707A was the first of the group to be fitted with leading edge intakes, which would later be used for the Vulcan. The sole 707C was a trainer featuring a side-by-side seating arrangement that was very cramped. A fly-by-wire electric servo system was later installed in the 707C for trials with the RAE at Bedford.

Service

Avro 707 VX784 completed its maiden flight from Boscombe Down in the hands of A&AEE's deputy chief test pilot, Sqn Ldr Lt Eric Elser DFC on 4 September 1949. After appearing on static display at the SBAC, Farnborough, VX784 was lost on 30 September after stalling near Blackbushe airport, taking the life of Elser with it. The Avro 707B was first flown on 6 September 1950 by Avro chief test pilot 'Roly' Falk, again in time to appear at the SBAC. Designed to operate at lower speeds to test the characteristics of delta wings, the 707B would contribute more valuable data for the development of the Vulcan than all of the other machines put together.

The third aircraft, 707A WD280, made its maiden flight from Boscombe Down on 14 June 1951; this machine was accurately described as a 'mini-Vulcan' because of its scaled down Type 698 wings. WD280 was also used to trial the famous kink that would be introduced in the leading edge of the Vulcan's wing. The final variant was the two-seater 707C WZ744, which did not contribute to the Vulcan programme but served with the A&AEE and RAE until early 1967.

Production

Five aircraft were built, beginning with 707 VX784; this was followed by 707B VX790, 707A WD280; 707A WZ736 and 707C WZ744. Both WZ736 and WZ744 were built at Bracebridge Heath and first flown from Waddington.

Technical data - 707, A, B & C	
ENGINE	(707 & 707B) One 3,500lb Rolls-Royce Derwent 5; (707A & 707C) One 3,600lb Rolls-Royce Derwent 8
WINGSPAN	(707 & B) 33ft; (707A & C) 34ft 2in
LENGTH	(707) 30ft 6in; (707A, B & C) 42ft 4in
HEIGHT	(707A & C) 11ft 7in; (707B) 11ft 9in
LOADED WEIGHT	(707) 8,600lb; (707A & B) 9,500lb; (707C) 10,000lb

Right: The third 707 built was 707A WD280, which was first flown by Wg Cdr 'Roly' Falk from Boscombe Down on 14 June 1951. The aircraft was designed to be operated at the highest possible subsonic speed. (*Aeroplane*)

Below: Both Vulcan prototypes, VX770 and VX777, accompanied by the four surviving 707s, head towards the Sussex coast with RAF Thorney Island in the background. (*Aeroplane*)

706 Ashton Mk 1 to 4

Development

As good an aircraft as it was, the Tudor Mk 8's tail-dragger undercarriage arrangement was not conducive to jet power. Redesigned with a tricycle undercarriage, an order was placed by the Air Ministry for six Tudor Mk 9s. Based on the Tudor Mk II airliner, the aircraft was later renamed as the Ashton, an aircraft that would become the most successful product from a very troubled dynasty.

Design

Converted from the thicker-skinned Tudor Mk II airframe, the Ashton was a good-looking aircraft. The nose was extended with a false section, the lower part creating a bay for the nose wheel undercarriage. Power was provided by four Rolls-Royce Nene turbojets, neatly enclosed within a pair of long streamlined pods mounted under each wing. The main undercarriage retracted between the tail pipes, and the tall angular fin and rudder was another unique feature.

The pressure cabin of the first two aircraft was from a standard Tudor Mk II, while the remainder had a shorter cabin that ended forward of the main entrance door. The six aircraft all differed in very subtle ways, especially with regard to internal equipment depending on what trials they were involved with.

Service

The sole Ashton Mk 1, WB490, was the first aircraft to fly in the hands of Jimmy Orrell from Woodford on 1 September 1950. This aircraft went on to carry out high altitude research with the A&AEE at Boscombe Down. The only Mk 2 built, WB491, made its maiden flight on 2 August 1951 and served the RAE for pressurisation, refrigeration, humidification and temperature control investigation. Later converted by Napier as a test bed, WB491 trialled a Rolls-Royce Avon and Conway in a ventral pod.

The first of three Mk 3s was WB492, first flown on 6 July 1951 and delivered to the RRE at Defford for radar bombing trials. WB493 followed on 18 December 1951 for service with the RAE and later with Bristol at Filton to trial the Olympus and Orpheus. The final Mk 3, serialled out of sequence as WE670, was first flown on 9 April 1952; this aircraft being used for bomb ballistics research with the RAE. Later converted by Napier, WE670 became a test bed for the Rolls-Royce Avon RA.14, again mounted under the fuselage.

The Mk 4, WB494, was first flown on 11 November 1952 and featured a pressurised ventral bomb-aimer's pannier and bomb containers under the outer wing panels. After service with the RAE, the aircraft conducted Sapphire de-icing trials until February 1959.

The Ashton fleet contributed a great deal to the future of jet powered airliners, all being capable of remaining at altitude for much longer than previous test aircraft, not to mention providing a comfortable working environment for the flight test observers. One aircraft, WB493, was captured on film for posterity in the 1960 British film *Cone of Silence* in a plot line that followed a similar path to the early troubles of the Comet.

Production

Six aircraft were built at Woodford between 1949 and 1952; one Mk I (WB490), one Mk 2 (WB491), three Mk 3s (WB492, WB493 and WE670) and one Mk 4 (WB494).

Technical data – 706 Ashton Mk 1 to 4	
ENGINE	Four 5,000lb Rolls-Royce Nene 5 or 6
WINGSPAN	120ft
LENGTH	89ft 6½in
HEIGHT	31ft 3in
WING AREA	1,421 sq ft
LOADED WEIGHT	(Mk 1) 72,000lb
CRUISING SPEED	406mph
MAX SPEED	439mph

Right: The second Ashton to fly was Mk 3 WB492, seen here during its tenure with the RRE (Royal Radar Establishment), operating from Defford and Pershore. (*Aeroplane*)

Below: The first of just six Avro Ashtons built was WB490, posing for the camera during the early part of its flying career in December 1950, during which time it sported a large Hawker Siddeley Group logo on the nose. (*FLIGHT* via *Aeroplane*)

696 Shackleton MR Mk 2 & T Mk 2

Development

Considering the Shackleton MR Mk 1 entered service in February 1951 and was operational by the following month, the second version of the maritime reconnaissance aircraft was not long in the waiting. Feedback from the crews quickly highlighted areas of improvement, which Avro responded to by producing the revised MR Mk 2.

Design

The MR Mk 2 represented a major makeover of the type, and, following an extension of the nose and revised rear observers position in place of the rear gunner, the aircraft was almost 10ft longer than the MR Mk 1. The nose was more aerodynamic than its predecessors and was furnished with a front gunner's position with a pair of 20mm cannons. Below was the bomb-aimers location with a large optically flat glass panel. The radar was upgraded and repositioned in a large semi-retractable dustbin-type radome with 360-degree coverage, mounted in the lower fuselage aft of the wing. The MR Mk 2 was also fitted with a pair of retractable tailwheels.

Continually upgraded throughout its service career, the MR Mk 2 saw modifications to its engines, electronics and accommodation that resulted in Phase 1, 2 and 3 sub-variants. The MR Mk 2 Phase 3 featured new navigation and offensive equipment and a revised exhaust system that removed the soot trails from the upper wings. These were unofficially designated as the MR Mk 2C and were exclusively operated by 204 and 205 squadrons in Madagascar and the Far East, respectively.

Service

The MR Mk 2 modifications were first trialled by prototype VW126, the aircraft being fitted with dummy nose, tail fairings and radar and used as an aerodynamic test bed. The prototype MR Mk 2 was WB833, which was a MR Mk 1 removed from the production line, the aircraft flying for the first time on 17 June 1952.

Technical data – 696 Shackleton MR Mk 2	
ENGINE	Four 2,450hp Rolls-Royce Griffon 57A
WINGSPAN	120ft
LENGTH	87ft 3in
HEIGHT	16ft 9in
WING AREA	1,421 sq ft
EMPTY WEIGHT	54,200lb
LOADED WEIGHT	86,000lb
MAX SPEED	300mph at 18,300ft
SERVICE CEILING	25,700ft
RANGE	3,800 miles at 200mph

The MR Mk 2 first entered service with 42 Squadron at St Eval in January 1953, which retained the type until June 1966. The MR Mk 2 also served with the following operational squadrons: 37 (July 1953 to September 1967), 38 (September 1953 to March 1967), 120 (April 1953 to August 1954 and October 1956 to November 1958), 203 (April 1962 to December 1966), 204 (January 1954 to May 1958 and April 1971 to April 1972), 205 (February 1962 to October 1971), 206 (February 1953 to June 1954), 210 (December 1958 to October 1970 and November 1970 to November 1971), 220 (March 1953 to July 1954 and March to October 1957), 224 (May 1953 to October 1966), 228 (July 1954 to March 1959), 240 (March 1953 to August 1954) and 269 Squadron (March 1953 to August 1954 and October to November 1958).

The type supported a wide range of British operations across the globe throughout the 1950s, '60s and into the early '70s, including humanitarian missions. The aircraft was retired on 1 May 1972, when the Majunga detachment, supplied by the temporarily reformed 204 Squadron, was disbanded at Honington.

Production

In total, 69 Shackleton MR Mk 2s were built by Avro at Woodford between September 1952 and January 1955 in the serial ranges WG530 to WG558, WL737 to WL801 and WR951 to WR969. Ten aircraft were converted to T Mk 2 standard, serialled WG533, WG554, WG558, WL739, WL750, WL787, WR964, WR966, WR967 and WR969.

First production Shackleton MR Mk 2 WB833 first flew from Woodford on 17 June 1952. The aircraft undertook extensive trials throughout its career until 1966 when the aircraft was allocated to 210 Squadron at Ballykelly Wing. This Shackleton was lost on 19 April 1968, when it crashed on the Mull of Kintyre during a naval exercise in poor weather conditions. (*Aeroplane*)

A pristine quartet of 228 Squadron MR Mk 2s, formatting for the camera not long after the unit was re-formed at St Eval on 1 July 1954. (*Aeroplane*)

716 Shackleton MR Mk 3

Development
Once again designed in response to operational experience, the final maritime reconnaissance variant of the Shackleton was the Mk 3, which like its predecessor would be constantly updated throughout its service career but would serve no longer than it. The type was also introduced in response to the withdrawal of the Sunderland and the final transfer of all Coastal Command operations to land-based aircraft.

Design
The most obvious single change introduced by the MR Mk 3 was the undercarriage configuration, which was changed from a tail dragger to a tricycle arrangement. The increased all-up weight of the aircraft also saw an increase in wheels; the main units and nose wheels all having a pair apiece. The MR Mk 3 had to match the impressive range of the Sunderland and to achieve this a pair of auxiliary fuel tanks was fitted to the wing tips, raising the total amount of fuel carried to 4,248 gallons. The cockpit was installed with a clear-vision frameless canopy and internally sound-proofing was improved, as was the galley and sleeping area to help the crew cope with sorties lasting, on average, 18 hours.

The same updates the MR Mk 2 was subjected to were also applied to the MR Mk 3, beginning with Phase 1, which saw changes to internal equipment; Phase 2 introduced ECM equipment, better HF radio and diesel exhaust detection equipment and Phase 3, because of the increasing weight, involved the fitment of two Viper turbojet engines into the rear of the outboard engine nacelles to help get the 100,000lb aircraft off the runway.

Service
The MR Mk 3 first entered RAF service with 220 Squadron at St Mawgan in August 1957 but only served until October 1958, when the unit was disbanded. The aircraft also served with 42 (November 1965 to September 1971), 120 (September 1958 to February 1971), 201 (October 1958 to December 1970),

Technical data – 716 Shackleton MR Mk 3	
ENGINE	Four 2,450hp Rolls-Royce Griffon 57A; (Phase 3) Plus two 2,500lb Bristol Siddeley Viper 203 auxiliary turbojets
WINGSPAN	119ft 10in
LENGTH	92ft 6in
HEIGHT	23ft 4in
WING AREA	1,458 sq ft
EMPTY WEIGHT	64,300lb
LOADED WEIGHT	100,000lb
MAX SPEED	302mph at 18,300ft
MAX CRUISING SPEED	253mph
INITIAL CLIMB RATE	850ft/min
SERVICE CEILING	19,200ft
RANGE	3,660 miles at 200mph at 1,500ft

203 (December 1958 to July 1962 and June 1966 to December 1971) and 206 squadrons (January 1958 to October 1970). 203 Squadron, based at Luqa, was the last RAF unit to operate the MR Mk 3, when it was retired in favour of the Nimrod MR Mk 1 in December 1971.

The MR Mk 3 achieved the only overseas sales of the Shackleton when the SAAF received the first of eight examples on 18 August 1957. Serving solely with 35 Squadron throughout their long careers, the SAAF did not withdraw the MR Mk 3 until 1984, and only then because the airframes were life-expired with an average of 10,000 hours on each. One of the SAAF machines, 1716 *Pelican 16*, was famously restored back to flight in 1994, only to crash land in the Western Sahara, where it remains to this day.

Production

A single prototype, WR970, was built, plus 34 production MR Mk 3s built between September 1956 and May 1959 in the serial ranges WR970 to WR990, XF700 to XF711 and XF730. Eight MR Mk 3 were delivered to the SAAF between August 1957 and February 1958 with serials 1716 to 1723.

Right: Prototype Shackleton MR Mk 3 WR970 first flew from Woodford on 2 September 1955. After trials with the A&AEE at Boscombe Down, the aircraft was lost during a test flight from Woodford on 7 December 1956, killing Avro test pilot Jack B Wales DFC, OBE, TD and his three crew. (*Aeroplane*)

Below: A pair of 201 Squadron Shackleton MR Mk 3s are operating out of St Mawgan, circa 1963–64. Nearest to the camera is WR977, which went on to serve with 42 and 203 squadrons until it was allocated to Thorney Island as a fire trainer in November 1971. This decision was reversed, and after spending many years at Finningley, the aircraft was dismantled and delivered by road to the Newark Air Museum on 1 May 1977. (Martyn Chorlton)

698 Vulcan, B Mk 1 & B Mk 1A

Development

The world's first large bomber to use a delta-wing, the Vulcan, began life as an Air Staff Requirement in 1946 that had evolved into specification B.35/46 by the following year. The remit was simple; produce a high-altitude bomber capable of carrying a nuclear war load at a speed approaching Mach 1. Roy Chadwick laid the foundation blocks for the design, which was accepted on November 27, 1947; sadly, the great designer was killed before this momentous day arrived.

Design

Despite its dramatic external appearance, the structure of the Vulcan followed traditional rules, including a twin-spar wing, rearward retracting nose gear, forward retracting main undercarriage and four Avon (later Olympus) engines grouped close together near the centreline. Of all-metal, stressed skin construction, the main feature was the colossal wing, which was 7ft thick at the root. The wing accommodated the engines, undercarriage, the entire bomb load, and fuel tanks easily within its confines. A conventional rudder was mounted on the rear of a swept fin, and all other flying controls, consisting of two pairs of ailerons and elevators were assembled on the trailing edge of the wing. Flaps were deemed unnecessary because of the high angle of attack when landing and gate-type airbrakes could be extended above and below the wing plus a large brake parachute, ensuring that the Vulcan could be brought to a halt quickly.

Technical data – Vulcan prototypes & B Mk 1	
ENGINE	(VX770) Four 6,500lb Rolls-Royce Avon RA.3, four 8,000lb Armstrong Siddeley Sapphire or four Rolls-Royce Conway R.Co.7; (VX777) Four 9,750lb Bristol Olympus 100; (B Mk 1) Four 11,000lb Bristol Olympus 101, 12,000lb Olympus 102 or 13,000lb Olympus 104
WINGSPAN	99ft
LENGTH	97ft 1in
HEIGHT	26ft 6in
WING AREA	3,554 sq ft
LOADED WEIGHT	170,000lb
MAX SPEED	625mph at 36,000ft
CRUISING SPEED	607mph at 50,000ft
SERVICE CEILING	55,000ft
RANGE	3,000 miles
ARMAMENT	21 conventional 1,000lb bombs or a variety of nuclear bombs including Blue Danube, Red Beard, Violet Club and Yellow Sun

Service

The first prototype, serialled VX770, powered by four Avons, made its maiden flight from Woodford on 30 August 1952 followed by the second, Olympus-powered VX777, on 3 September 1953. In RAF service, the first aircraft were designated as the B Mk 1, and the first of these joined 230 OCU at Waddington in May 1956.

83 Squadron at Waddington became the first operational unit on 11 July 1957 (until August 1960) followed by 44 (August 1960 to September 1967), 50 (August 1961 to October 1966), 101 (October 1957 to December 1967) and 617 Squadron (May 1958 to July 1961). By 1961, a large number of B Mk 1s were upgraded to Mk 1As, which entailed the fitment of ECM equipment in an extended radome mounted on the rear of the fuselage. This variant remained in RAF service until December 1967, although from May 1961, 83 Squadron had already re-equipped with the B Mk 2.

The speed and ease with which the Vulcan could cover long distances was demonstrated early on, when XA897 left Boscombe Down on 9 September 1956 and landed in Melbourne just 23hrs 9mins later. This achievement was eclipsed by 617 Squadron in June 1961, when XH481 departed Scampton bound for Sydney. The 11,500-mile flight was carried out in 20hrs 3mins 17secs at an average speed of 573 mph.

Production

Two prototype Vulcans, serialled VX770 and VX777, were built, followed by 45 production B Mk 1s, all built at Woodford and serialled XA889 to ZA913, XH475 to XH483, XH497 to XH506 and XH532. The following aircraft were converted to B Mk 1A standard: XA895, XA900, XA901, XA904, XA906, XA907, XA909 to XA913, XH475 to XH483, XH497 to XH506 and XH532.

Right: The first production Avro Vulcan B Mk 1, XA889, arrives at Farnborough. Note the straight-edged pure delta plan form of the aircraft's wing, which was later revised from XA890 onwards into the 'Phase 2' design. This entailed a 52 to 42° sweepback at half span, giving the wing a distinctive kink, which was increased with the later B Mk 2. (Martyn Chorlton)

Below: The first RAF unit to receive the Vulcan B Mk 1 was 230 OCU, which was re-formed at Waddington on 31 May 1956. One of the first to arrive was XA895, with a tiny puff of smoke behind the nose wheel at the point of final touchdown at Waddington. (Martyn Chorlton)

698 Vulcan B Mk 2 & K Mk 2

Development

As the development and potential power of the Bristol Olympus series of engines gained momentum, Avro designers set to work on producing the next version of the Vulcan even though the B Mk 1 had only just entered production.

Design

It was the arrival of the 16,000lb Olympus 200 engine, first tested in B Mk 1 XA891, that suddenly realised the full potential of what the Vulcan airframe could handle. The B Mk 2 would have an increased wingspan and the capability to carry the Avro 'Blue Steel' stand-off bomb or the Douglas Skybolt missile. Harnessing the additional power resulted in a reduced thickness/chord ratio of the wing at its outer point and an increase in the compound taper of the leading edge. Elevons replaced the B Mk 1s conventional ailerons and elevators. This new wing arrangement was first flown by VX777 on 31 August 1957.

The first B Mk 2s to enter service were powered by the 17,000lb Olympus 201, which was later replaced by the excellent 20,000lb Olympus 301; the latter taking the Vulcan's performance to the aerodynamic limits of the aircraft. The B Mk 2 was also completely independent when it came to outside services, thanks to a Rover auxiliary power unit.

The operational range of the bomber was further increased by Valiant and later Victor tankers. This latter role was also undertaken by the Vulcan in 1982 when six were converted to K Mk 2 standard in response to the long-range operations conducted during the Falklands War.

Service

The Vulcan B Mk 2 first entered service with 230 OCU on 1 July 1960 and 83 Squadron from December 1960. The mark also served with 9 (April 1962 to April 1982), 12 (July 1962 to December 1967), 27 (April 1961 to March 1972), 35 (December 1962 to February 1982), 44 (September 1966 to December 1982), 50 (B Mk 2 January 1966 to March 1984 and K Mk 2 June 1982 to March 1984), 83 (December 1960 to August 1969), 101 (December 1967 to August 1982) and 617 Squadron (September 1961 to December 1981).

Capable of carrying a wide range of nuclear weapons, the B Mk 2 only hit the headlines in the twilight of its career when the epic Operation *Black Buck* took place on 1 May 1982. This incredible 6,800-mile, 16 hour-long operation was the longest bombing raid at the time, only eclipsed in 1991 by the USAF's B-52s operating from the US during the first Gulf War.

Production

In total, 89 Vulcan B Mk 2s were built at Woodford between September 1959 and January 1965 in the serial ranges XH533 to XH539, XH554 to XH563, XJ780 to XJ784, XJ823 to XJ825, XL317 to XL321, XL359 to XL361, XL384 to XL392, XL425 to XL427, XL443 to XL446, XM569 to XM576, XM594 to XM612 and XM645 to XM657. Six aircraft converted to K Mk 2 were XH558, XH560, XH561, XJ825, XL445 and XM571.

Technical data – Vulcan B Mk 2	
ENGINE	Four 16,000lb Bristol Olympus 200, 17,000lb Olympus 210 or 20,000lb Olympus 301
WINGSPAN	111ft
LENGTH	99ft 1in
HEIGHT	27ft 1in
WING AREA	3,964 sq ft
LOADED WEIGHT	200,000lb
MAX SPEED	645mph at 36,000ft
CRUISING SPEED	620mph at 55,000ft
SERVICE CEILING	60,000ft
RANGE	4,600 miles

Right: The most famous Vulcan of them all, XH558, during one its final sorties with RAF's Vulcan Display Flight in 1992. After a successful, but often nerve-racking, period of fund raising, XH558 was returned to the air on 18 October 2007. (*Aeroplane*)

Below: 617 Squadron Vulcan B Mk 2 XL321 carrying a Blue Steel standoff, supersonic cruise-type air-to-surface missile, which the unit introduced to service at Scampton in February 1963. Fitted with a Red Snow 1.1 Megaton warhead, the Blue Steel travelled, after launch, at Mach 2.5 towards its target. The weapon was withdrawn from service in 1970 in favour of Polaris. (Martyn Chorlton)

698 Vulcan Test Beds

Testing from the outset

The Vulcan was involved in engine testing for over 20 years, the type ably assisting the British jet engine manufacturing industry to shakedown a wide range powerplants not only for the bomber itself, but also ground-breaking types such as the TSR.2, Tornado and even Concorde.

The aircraft

The first of eight Vulcan test beds was the prototype VX770, which was designed with the Olympus in mind, but was destined never to be fitted with the engine. Instead, the bomber's Avon RA.3s was replaced by a quartet of Armstrong Siddeley Sapphire SA.6 turbojets purely for the Vulcan's own development from 1953. By 1956, the aircraft was refitted with four 15,000lb Conway R.Co.7 engines, which, in upgraded form, would power the Victor. The aircraft performed valuable work with the A&AEE and Rolls-Royce until it was lost at Syerston in September 1958.

The first production B Mk 1, XA899, was initially trialled with the 12,000lb Olympus 102 and later the 13,500lb Olympus 104, both of which were cleared for use for the production aircraft. B Mk 1 XA891 also served as a Vulcan engine development aircraft when it trialled four 16,000lb Olympus 200 engines in 1958. XA891 was lost on 24 July 1959 following a major electrical fault climbing out of Woodford. The bomber, flown by Jimmy Harrison, was successfully abandoned by all five crew before crashing at High Hunsley, Walkington, near Beverley.

B Mk 1 XA894 was a dedicated non-Vulcan engine test bed, which was powered by four Olympus 101s plus an Olympus 320 in an underslung pod with a bifurcated intake. The engine was being trialled for the BAC TSR.2, but sadly the aircraft was a total loss after it caught fire on the ground at Filton on 3 December 1962. B Mk 1 XA896 was also involved in another ill-fated project after it was withdrawn from RAF service in June 1964 to trial the Bristol Siddeley BS.100 vectored thrust engine for the HS P.1154. The aircraft was cancelled in February 1965, and, before conversion had been completed, XA896 was scrapped.

Another Vulcan withdrawn from RAF service was ex-230 OCU, B Mk 1 XA902, which replaced VX770 as a Conway test bed. A 1,000 hour-long Conway R.Co.11 test was completed by XA902, and later the bomber trialled a pair of Spey engines in the inboard and a pair of Conway engines in the outboard positions. In this configuration, XA902 first flew from Hucknall on 12 October 1961. The Spey development work went on to benefit the DH Trident, BAC One-Eleven and Blackburn/HS Buccaneer S Mk 2.

The longest serving Vulcan test bed of all was XA903, which was converted in the same way as XA894 with a large underslung pod. This time, though, the pod contained an Olympus 593 for Concorde, and after its maiden flight with this unit, XA903 carried out 400 hours of test-flying between 1 October 1966 and June 1971. Two years later, XA903 was employed again, this time with an exact replica of the starboard half of Tornado complete with an RB.199 turbofan. First flown in April 1973, the RB.199 was fitted with both reheat and thrust reverse capability. After 285 hours of flight testing with the RB.199, XA903 became the last B Mk 1 to fly when it landed at Farnborough for the final time on 1 March 1979.

The sole B Mk 2 test bed was XH557, which was employed by Bristol Siddeley to test the definitive 20,000lb Olympus 301 engine in May 1961. Returned to RAF service in 1965, the bomber was retired in December 1982.

Technical data – 698 Vulcan test beds	
ENGINES	(all aircraft) 8,000lb Sapphire; 15,000lb Conway R.Co.7 & R.Co.11; 12,000lb Olympus 102; 20,000lb Olympus 301; 22,000lb (dry), 30,610lb (wet); Olympus 320; 20,000lb (dry), 30,610lb (wet); Olympus 593; 8,700lb (dry), 14,840lb (wet) RB.199 Mk 101

The third production Vulcan B Mk1, XA891, was used to trial the 16,000lb Olympus 200 engine in 1958. However, the testing was destined to be short-lived as the bomber was lost on 24 July 1959, after a major electrical fault and subsequent total engine failure. (Martyn Chorlton)

XA894 makes a low pass at Farnborough, showing off its Olympus 320 engine and bifurcated air intakes. The engine was being trialled for the ill-fated British Aircraft Corporation (BAC) TSR.2. (Martyn Chorlton)

748MF (780) Andover C MK 1, CC Mk 2 & E Mk 3/3A

Development

A successful development of the civilian Avro 748 short- to medium-range feederliner, a military variant of this excellent aircraft was not long in the waiting. In response to an RAF requirement for a medium tactical freighter, the Dart-powered Avro 748MF (Military Freighter) went head-to-head with a proposed military variant of the Handley Page Dart Herald.

Design

An orthodox-looking aircraft, the 748MF was an all-metal, low-wing fully pressurised machine with a circular-section fuselage. The key features of the military variant were a redesigned upswept rear fuselage with a rear loading door and a high dihedral tailplane. Power was provided by two Dart R.Da.12 turboprops driving a pair of large 14ft 6in-diameter Dowty-Rotol propellers. The floor was reinforced to handle wheeled vehicles up to Land Rover size and to maintain the rear loading at the same level of the floor, the undercarriage could be lowered into a kneeling position. The 'MF' could be presented in a wide range of layouts, including 40 paratroops, 48 troops and equipment or as a casualty evacuation aircraft for 15 walking wounded and 18 stretcher cases.

Service

The MF programme moved swiftly, because the HS.748 prototype, G-APZV, was converted instead of building a new aircraft, and in its new form first flew from Woodford on 21 December 1963 as the 748MF prototype (internally designated as the Avro 780), reregistered as G-ARRV. The first production

Technical data – Andover C Mk 1	
ENGINE	(C Mk 1) Two 3,245ehp Rolls-Royce Dart RDa 12 Mk 201C turboprops
WINGSPAN	90ft
LENGTH	77ft 11in
HEIGHT	30ft 1in
WING AREA	831 sq ft
EMPTY WEIGHT	27,709lb
LOADED WEIGHT	44,500lb
MAX SPEED	302mph at 15,000ft
CRUISING SPEED	258mph at 20,000ft
SERVICE CEILING	23,800ft
MAX RANGE	2,700 miles with overload fuel tanks

C Mk 1, XS594, now named Andover, first flew on 9 July 1965, and after acceptance trials at the A&AEE, the type entered service with 46 Squadron in September 1966. The RAF also took delivery of the CC MK 2, based on the HS.748 Series 2 and later several C Mk 1s were converted to E Mk 3/3A standard furnished with special electronic equipment.

The Andover served with the following RAF units – 21 (CC Mk 2 February to September 1967), 32 (C Mk 1 September 1975 to 1993, CC Mk 2 February 1969 to 31 March 1995), 46 (C Mk 1 September 1966 to August 1975), 52 (C Mk 1 December 1966 to December 1969), 60 (C Mk 1 April 1987 to March 1992, CC Mk 2 October 1971 to November 1975 and March 1987 to March 1992), 84 (C Mk 1 August 1967 to September 1971) and 115 Squadron (E Mk 3/3A November 1976 to October 1993) and 241 and 242 OCU, A&AEE, Andover Conversion Unit, ETPS, The Queen's Flight and the RAE.

Ten ex-RAF Andovers were sold to the RNZAF in 1976 and were not retired until 1998. In Britain, the last Andover, XS646, was only withdrawn from use early in 2013.

Production (RAF only)
One prototype, serialled G-AARV, was built, followed by 31 production Andover C Mk 1s serialled XS594 to XS597, XS598 to XS613 and XS637 to XS647. Six Andover CC Mk 2s were built, serialled XS789 to XS794. Four C Mk 1s were converted to E Mk 3 serialled XS603, XS605, XS610 and XS640, plus four to E Mk 3A standard, serialled XS639, XS641, XS643 and XS644.

Right: **Two Andover CC Mk 2s, XS789 and XS790, served with The Queen's Flight and later 32 (Royal) Squadron into the 1990s. Based on the civilian HS.748 Series 2, the interiors were laid out in standard passenger configuration. (Martyn Chorlton)**

Below: **XS639 was one of eight C Mk 1s converted to E Mk 3/3A standard to take over the electronic duties of the Argosy E Mk 1 serving with 115 Squadron at Brize Norton and later Benson. Their tasking was to undertake radio and airport navigation calibration duties until they were withdrawn in October 1993. (Martyn Chorlton)**

696 Shackleton AEW Mk 2

Development

As senior RAF staff prepared for the complete withdrawal of the Shackleton from the inventory, a sudden void appeared in Britain's Airborne Early Warning (AEW) network with the simultaneous retirement of the FAA Gannet AEW Mk 3s. This, combined with the scrapping of HMS *Ark Royal*, meant that an alternative needed to found, and quickly; the Shackleton proved to be the perfect aircraft for the job.

Design

The idea of modifying the Shackleton into an AEW aircraft was first discussed in 1967, and not long after, the MR Mk 2 was deemed as the most suitable airframe for the job. The first of 12 conversions began in 1970, the main task being the installation of the Gannet's large AN/APS-20(F) radar (developed for the Avenger in 1946!) and its equally cumbersome ventral radome mounted on the underside of the fuselage, directly below the cockpit. The conversion work was carried out by HSA at Bitteswell, while the radar was actually installed by RAF engineers at Lossiemouth.

Service

The first aircraft, WL745, made its maiden flight as an AEW Mk 2 from Woodford on 30 September 1971. All AEW Mk 2s were destined to serve with 8 Squadron, which was re-formed at Kinloss on 1 January 1972, by then the only RAF unit to fly the Shackleton operationally, and because of the amount of manpower needed it was the largest squadron in the RAF. All of the aircraft were subsequently named after the main characters in the *Magic Roundabout* and *The Herbs*.

The long-term plan was to replace the Shackleton with the Nimrod AEW Mk 3 by the early 1980s, but this never came about and the AEW Mk 2 was forced to soldier on into the early 1990s. For almost 20 years, 8 Squadron's 12 crews remained at high-readiness 24 hours a day, seven days a week. The

Technical data – 696 Shackleton AEW Mk 2	
ENGINE	Four 2,450hp Rolls-Royce Griffon 57A
WINGSPAN	120ft
LENGTH	87ft 3in
HEIGHT	16ft 9in
WING AREA	1,421 sq ft
EMPTY WEIGHT	54,200lb
LOADED WEIGHT	86,000lb
MAX SPEED	300mph at 18,300ft
SERVICE CEILING	25,700ft
RANGE	3,800 miles at 200mph

Shackleton, held in affection by many, was far from being the most comfortable aircraft to work in for hours on end; the noise alone was a test of character, not to mention the cold aggravated by the unpressurised fuselage and inefficient petrol fired heating system. Regardless, the crews performed sterling work in an aircraft that remained in service for many years longer than planned.

On 30 June 1991, the Shackleton was finally retired from the RAF's inventory, causing a tear or two for the enthusiast, relief for the ground engineers and a future for the aircrew flying the state-of-the-art Sentry AEW Mk 1.

Production

Twelve AEW Mk 2s were converted from standard MR Mk 2s between August 1970 and August 1972, serialled and christened as WL741 *PC Knapweed*, WL745 *Sage*, WL747 *Florence*, WL754 *Paul*, WL756 *Mr Rusty*, WL757 *Brian*, WL790 *Mr McHenry* (later *Zebedee*), WL793 *Ermintrude*, WL795 *Rosalie*, WR960 *Dougal*, WR963 *Parsley* (later *Ermintrude*) and WR965 *Dill* (later *Rosalie II*).

Above: First flown as a MR Mk 2 on 18 March 1952, WL754 served with 37, 38, 42, 204 and 205 squadrons before it was converted into an AEW Mk 2 in 1972. The aircraft, named *Paul*, served with 8 Squadron until 1981 when it was withdrawn from service, flown to Valley where it was used as a fire trainer and later scrapped. (*Aeroplane*)

Right: A classic 'what could have been' photograph of Shackleton AEW Mk 2 WR960 *Dougal* and its intended replacement, a Nimrod AEW Mk 3, banking away beyond. The Nimrod AEW was cancelled in 1987, by which time the government had already approached Boeing, and the future of 8 Squadron was sealed. (Martyn Chorlton)

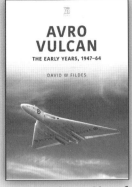

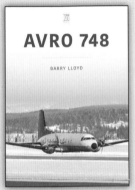